THE RENAISSANCE OF ITALIAN GARDENS

Lorenza de' Medici

THE RENAISSANCE OF ITALIAN GARDENS

PHOTOGRAPHS BY JOHN FERRO SIMS

Fawcett Columbine · New York

A Fawcett Columbine Book
Published by Ballantine Books

Text copyright © 1990 by Lorenza de'Medici
Text in association with Giuppi Pietromarchi
Photographs copyright © 1990 by John Ferro Sims

Library of Congress Cataloging-in-Publication Data

De'Medici, Lorenza.
The Renaissance of Italian gardens/Lorenza de'Medici:
photographs by John Ferro Sims.
p.   cm.
ISBN 0–449–90441–5
1. Gardens, Italian.   2. Gardens, Renaissance – Italy.
3. Gardens – Italy.   4. Gardens, Italian – Pictorial works.
5. Gardens, Renaissance – Italy – Pictorial works.
6. Gardens – Italy – Pictorial works.   I. Sims, John Ferro.   II. Title.
SB457.85.D4 1990   89–78422
712'.0945'09024–dc20   CIP

Designed by Bernard Higton

Manufactured in Italy

First American Edition: September 1990

10 9 8 7 6 5 4 3 2 1

PHOTOGRAPHS

Page One: The main avenue of Cherry laurel and linden trees
leading to Marocco di Venezia, Nuvoletti.
Page Two: *Acer palmatum atropurpureum* at Marocco di Venezia
Page Five: The Pompeiian Garden, Villa Polissena.

ACKNOWLEDGEMENTS

I wish to thank Giuppi Pietromarchi for her invaluable
collaboration and expertise throughout the project.
I also wish to thank Shanti Evans for the excellent translation
and all those people who so graciously opened their
gardens for the pleasure of our readers.

CONTENTS

INTRODUCTION

This book represents a quest in search of some of the great gardens of the past that have been recreated and brought back to life in recent years, gardens in which those elements that have always been a feature of the traditional Italian garden, but that have faded or fallen into dereliction over the last few centuries, have been reinstated and restored to their former prominence.

During the Renaissance the concept of the garden began to acquire a new emphasis, one whose spirit was based on the patrician ideal of country life that had reached its fullest expression in imperial Rome; the architectural form of the garden that was developed at this time was however, wholly original. The first great Renaissance gardens were created by Cosimo de'

ABOVE: A BEAUTIFUL VIEW OF CAPRI FROM A TERRACE AT LO STUDIO.
LEFT: THE SOUTHERN END OF THE PARTERRE, CASTEL GANDOLFO.

Medici – at Cafaggiolo in 1451, and later at Fiesole – and shortly afterwards, work began on the Vatican gardens in Rome, at the behest of Pope Nicholas V. Lorenzo de' Medici introduced the fashion for adorning gardens with statues (as, for example, in the Piazza San Marco in Florence), while Leon Battista Alberti laid down his precepts concerning the essential harmony that must exist between the architectural lines of the house and the design of the garden.

Pope Julius II commissioned Bramante to lay out for him the magnificent arrangement of statuary in the Villa del Belvedere, next to the Vatican palace, and to build its two monumental loggias and an open-air theater, inspired by the Roman ruins of Preneste.

It was Bramante who took the Italian Renaissance garden to the peak of its development, formulating new ideas that were to have an enormous influence over the architectural evolution of the entire period, as is evident, for example, in the garden of the Villa di Fassolo, in Genoa, created for Andrea Doria by Montorsoli.

The most important gardens of the second half of the sixteenth century were almost all laid out in Rome: the Farnese gardens designed by Vignola for Pope Paul III on the slopes of the Palatine Hill, the Villa Medici built by Annibale Lippi for Cardinal Ricci on the Pincio, and the Villa d'Este at Tivoli on which Pirro Ligorio worked for thirty years. With these and innumerable other examples of sixteenth-century gardens there was a gradual shift towards the park, as at the villa of Francesco de' Medici, where the gardens were redesigned by Bernardo Buontalenti and divided into two parts, precise geometric symmetry giving way to freer forms and greater expressiveness. This was a prelude to the gardens of the seventeenth century, as exemplified by the large country houses in the Veneto, along the banks of the river Brenta and in the area of Treviso. Over the course of the next hundred years, the creative impetus of the Italian garden began to slacken. From the middle of the eighteenth to the end of the nineteenth century, the Italian tradition was abandoned in favor of the imitation of English-style landscaped gardens. This vogue had particularly deleterious effects in Italy, where ancient gardens were irrevocably altered, traditional layouts obliterated and statues mutilated, and that balance of volumes, spaces and geometric elegance on which the charm of the Italian garden had largely depended was almost entirely destroyed.

It was not until the 1950s and 1960s that an interest in gardens began to revive in Italy. Two different reasons, which were often combined, accounted for this revival. The first was a cultural one, a desire to restore, wherever possible, the Renaissance garden to its ancient splendor, and the second a purely botanical one, based on a love of plants and flowers. The rebirth of the Italian garden has been brought about by a new generation of passionate and dedicated gardeners whose intelligence, enthusiasm, and farsightedness has led to the creation of many of the gardens presented here. They are uniquely Italian gardens, some of them based on the traces of ancient history, others inspired by a unique blend of the Mediterranean landscape and light, all of them the result of research, imagination, and a deep feeling for the world of plants.

Writing this book I had no pretensions to making a work of history, and still less be didactic in any horticultural sense: it is a book written for people with a passion for gardens, who will happily drive for hours through the rain or walk miles across sun-baked fields in the hope of discovering a corner of paradise. The search for new plants and new ideas is a source of incomparable joy, and, most important of all, it provides the strength and motivation to revive gardens whose soul has long been neglected or forgotten. To take in hand an old, abandoned garden is one of the most enthralling experiences that life can offer us: to liberate trees that have been suffocated by ivy, to discover ancient foundations concealed beneath the earth, and to strip away the centuries and restore life to something buried is infinitely exciting and rewarding. As one's hands gradually bring the old remains to light, ideas take shape, and the imagination which will give life to the new garden is born, taking over from the spirit of its predecessor and reflecting the needs, tastes, and personality of its new owner.

It must not be forgotten that the Italian gardens of today are largely the result of experimentation with plants that have been little used up to now. Their designs are flexible and very often improvised, rarely following any pre-ordained pattern. Italy is lucky in having sun and water in abundance, which allows Italian gardeners freedom to express themselves in a variety of ways: the garden is often seen as a stage, where the scenery changes according to the work that is being performed and the flowers and plants are moved around like the characters in a play.

The aim of this book is to discover not only the enormous range of gardens that exist in Italy but also the influences that have made them what they are.

In Sicily, the garden of Principe and Principessa Borghese shows how the environment, climate, and plants of the southern Mediterranean can provide a perfect setting for a profusion of flowering plants and trees, while on Capri the theatrical costume designer Umberto Tirelli has devised a sumptuous display of color and texture in order to clothe the bare rocks of his spectacular island garden.

In Lazio the landscape and natural vegetation becomes gentler: the garden of Principe Enrico d'Assia is inimitably Roman in its rather fanciful thirties' style and its collection of ancient statues recalling the gardens of classical antiquity; and in the countryside near Rome Marchesa Lavinia Taverna Gallarati Scotti has created a garden that changes with almost every season, like a botanical workshop in which new plants and new ideas are constantly being developed. In the parched Maremma, close to the border between Lazio and Tuscany, an area scorched by the sun in summer and lashed by winds from both north and south, an olive grove planted in the nineteenth century has been transformed by Contessa Giuppi Pietromarchi into a lush green island in a boundless sea of grain, like an atoll in the middle of the Pacific.

Further north, the gentle hills of the Chianti district of Tuscany – the heart of Renaissance Italy – provide an idyllic setting for gardens both old and new and for plant collections to delight the eye of the most expert horticulturist. My garden at Badia a Coltibuono is a shining example of a *hortus conclusus* that has been transformed into a modern garden without losing its soul: the ancient buildings have been adapted to provide a large open space for a delightful collection of plants and flowers that entwine the centuries-old abbey like a colored ribbon.

As one travels north, the influence of Romanticism begins to strengthen perceptibly, as if a faint Nordic mist lay like a blanket over the landscape and its gardens. The colors of Titian and Veronese derive from the soft tones of the earth of the Veneto, from the red of the sunset, the clear, sparkling light and the delicate intense green of the landscape, colors that are reflected in the garden at Rivella, near Padua, where Contessa Marina Emo Capodilista has created an entirely new setting, adorned with magnificent mixed borders, for her splendid Palladian villa.

A sweet atmosphere of melancholy pervades the gardens of the Lombardy lakes, such as that of the architect Pier Fausto Bagatti Valsecchi on Lake Como, which has been handed down from father to son. On Lake Garda, Professor Arturo Hruska has created a fascinating garden of Alpine plants inspired by the dramatic landscape of the Dolomites, while further southwest in Piedmont a barely perceptible hint of French influence can be detected in the methodical planting schemes and the rich abundance of flowers in gardens such as Inge Feltrinelli's, near Turin.

These are just a few of the gardens I explored in this journey through Italy: each of them has a personality of its own and a soul that mirrors the imagination of its owner. The great revival of the Italian garden is based in part on this individuality: it follows no set fashion or rules, but expresses in an infinite variety of ways the talents of this new breed of gardeners who have given it a new breath of life.

BADIA A COLTIBUONO

Amidst magnificent pine woods the
"hortus conclusus" of Piero Stucchi Prinetti
and Lorenza de' Medici

Years ago, when I was just engaged to marry my husband Piero Stucchi Prinetti, he proposed to show me his country home. We left Florence in the morning by car and made our way to the estate. Taking the winding road up from the little town of Gaiole in Chianti, it suddenly appeared to me in the distance, the breathtaking sight of Badia a Coltibuono, and time seemed to stand still as the magnificently preserved medieval abbey, surrounded by conifers, came into view.

As we crossed the main courtyard and walked into the garden, I recalled a description I had read recently, written by Francesco di Moncino, the Abbot of Coltibuono in 1427. As was customary among the clergy, his description

ABOVE: MAY VINE LEAVES ON THE VAULTED PERGOLA.
LEFT: LOOKING TOWARDS THE EAST WING OF THE HOUSE ALONG THE VAULTED PERGOLA
UNDERPLANTED WITH A BORDER OF 'FASHION' ROSES.

of his holdings was very modest and no doubt a deliberate underestimation:

"At said Abbey, close by the church, a kitchen-garden cum pergola, from which no fruit is obtained, save grapes for eating and not for wine, and cabbages, leeks, and salad; said place known as Coltibuono, its inhabitants and religious. Likewise at said Abbey large amount of woods made up of shrubs, that is broom, tree-heath, and there are some chestnuts. . . ."

A visit to the garden of Coltibuono, after reading its description by the wily abbot, reveals immediately just how well he had concealed its wonders. It takes much of its spirit from its monastic surroundings: detached from

A WINTER VIEW ACROSS THE GARDEN TOWARDS THE HOUSE.

the abbey, it lies – as the abbot said – "close by the church" and it is enclosed by walls which entirely exclude the surrounding countryside. A garden for prayer and contemplation, where the monks cultivated vegetables and vines ("cabbages, leeks, and salad") in the intervals between devotions, it was also a medicinal garden containing every kind of herb: lavender, sage, basil, marjoram, mint, tarragon, and rosemary, all those I use in my cooking today. At the beginning of this century, an Italian-style parterre with flowerbeds surrounded by box hedges was laid out in the central part of the garden,

which somehow blends in perfectly with its medieval surroundings, as if the peaceful harmony of the garden, set in its magnificent frame of fir and chestnut woods, has become inviolable over the centuries as a result of a love for plants which has been handed down from one generation to another.

The large *Magnolia grandiflora* was planted by Piero's great grandmother in the middle of the courtyard, below the flight of steps, and the still silence of the abbey seems to be concentrated under its cool green branches. On the hottest days of summer, all our friends love to sit in its dark shade, either to read or to take a siesta. A wisteria (*Wisteria floribunda*), and yellow Banksia roses, recently planted to completely cover the balustrade, enhance the tree's romantic setting with a typically nineteenth-century color scheme of lilac with a hint of yellow.

The sweet-smelling roses and wisteria run right along the balustrade below the house, yielding place, at the height of summer, to *Mandevilla suaveolens* and sky-blue *Plumbago auriculata*. After a bad frost which killed an old *Ryncospernum jasminoides*, I decided to cover a wall with a *Clematis montana rubens* and a 'Kiftsgate' rose, in order to enjoy its exquisite abundance of tiny white flowers. Every summer I love planting a mass of geraniums at the foot of the steps by the magnolia, ranging from the common zonal geranium to the one with scented leaves (*Pelargonium graveolens*), intermingled with white petunias. The terrace overlooks the Italian-style garden, which is lent charm by a profusion of 'Sea Foam' roses, whose name derives from the small white blooms like foaming water spurting from the sprays. Along the outer border, a hedge of pink lavender forms a delicate contrast to the box (*Buxus sempervirens*, a plant typical of formal "Italian gardens") and the roses. Lemon trees in antique earthenware vases stand in orderly rows in the lavender border. "Arbors of oranges citrons persimmons lemons and all other tasty fruits line the streets", runs one of the sonnets of Folgore da San Gemignano.

This garden of box trees is flanked by vaulted pergolas covered with vines:

TOWARDS THE WEST WING OF THE HOUSE ACROSS THE ITALIAN PARTERRE.

"It had around it and in a great part of the middle very broad paths, all straight as arrows and covered by pergolas of vines, which made great show of producing many grapes that year; and all then in flower gave off so great a scent through the garden, that mixed together with that of the many other things that anointed the garden, they seemed to be in the midst of all the spicery that ever grew in the Orient. . . ."

To add life and color, the paths of the pergolas have been planted with pink dahlias of medium height, and recently I interspersed these with 'Old Blush China' and 'Pinocchio' roses and lavender. I find the combination of red, pink, and lilac cheerful and very attractive.

A few years ago, always in search of "easy and generous" plants, I lined the base of the wall along the right side of the house with flower-covered masses of *Oenothera speciosa*, a small, hardy, and vigorous herbaceous perennial that blooms continuously from June to September. The bristly white flowers, with a yellow heart, look like myriads of white butterflies and they have the effect of softening the severity of the wall which is entirely covered by Virginia creeper *Parthenocissus*

ABOVE: THE POOLSIDE GARDEN FEATURING YELLOW BROOM
(CYTISUS SCOPARIUS) AND RUGOSA ROSES.
LEFT: THE ITALIAN PARTERRE IS SURROUNDED BY BOX HEDGES
AND WHITE ROSES 'SEA FOAM'.

A STRAWBERRY TREE (ARBUTUS UNEDO) AND HORTENSIAS.

quinquefolia. I am sure my generous Oenothera cannot be particular to Italian gardens, as so many friends from abroad who have visited Coltibuono have asked me for cuttings of this plant.

The last vine-covered path to the right leads to a garden of flowering shrubs: laid out in groups of three or four to produce a fine display during the flowering season, they include buddleia, spiraea, weigela, forsythia, kerria, *Philadelphus virginalis*, *Syringa vulgaris*, rhus, and mahonia. This small garden of delight has the virtue of flowering from spring to fall, as the plants have been chosen to ensure a continuous display over the months. The shrubbery is bordered by currant bushes, raspberries, gooseberries, which provide wonderful jams for my family and my cooking students, and 'Peace' roses.

Towards the great wood that encircles Coltibuono, are groups of *Camellia japonica*, azaleas, and rhododendrons. The shade and humidity of the wood, which extends from this corner of the upper garden, provide them with ideal conditions.

16

Another old pergola of vines takes us back to the vegetable garden, which I completely surrounded with varieties of aromatic herbs: rosemary, sage, thyme, sweet marjoram, many kinds of mint, balm, tarragon, lavender cotton, sorrel (*Rumex acetosa*), rue, and savory. Inside, the range of vegetables is extensive enough to produce a crop all the year round. To the right of the "kitchen garden cum pergola" is the lower garden, where an old pond is enclosed by a natural cloister formed by an immense cherry laurel, pruned to make a room with walls of greenery. From here there is a view over the woods and the hills beyond. A wall below, about ten meters in height, surrounds the new garden around the pool, which is reached either by means of a spiral staircase that runs down the wall surrounding the upper garden, or by a path that slopes gently down from the back of the garden on the right-hand side. This garden, on an almost abandoned plot of land, is really my own creation. Over the years I have planted in large groups so that the ground near the pool is now totally covered in a sea of yellow broom (*Cytisus scoparius*), shrubby cinquefoil, lavender cotton (*Santolina chamaecyparissus*), Rose of Sharon (*Hypericum calycinum*), and rosemary (*Rosmarinus lavandulaceus*). Along one side of the pool is a border made up of *Rugosa* roses such as 'Blanc Double de Coubert', 'Calocarpa', 'Frau Dagmar Hartopp', 'Pink Grootendorst', and 'Belinda' (hybrid Musk) while on the other is a cascade of 'Sea Foam' roses. Again there are patches of bay laurel, laurustinus, broom, *Juniperus horizontalis* 'Douglasii', and *Osmanthus fragrans*. Always keeping in mind how little water there is in summer, everything here has been worked out down to the smallest detail: colors, scents, times of flowering, shapes. Even fruit trees have been planted so that anyone emerging from the pool can sample a juicy apricot.

A few meters from the large well, an arbor of *Lonicera caprifolium* and *Polygonum cilinode* makes a cool shady place for summer lunches. Like some paradise on earth, the garden seems to be suspended between the Middle Ages and the twentieth century. I have taken great care in

A LARGE BED OF LAVENDER.

preserving its atmosphere while continually introducing innovations and new ideas, and thanks too to my success and luck in choosing plants well suited to the climate and the place, I hope I have succeeded in making a garden where all the fundamental principles of the medieval garden, the *hortus conclusus*, the Italian-style garden, and the garden set in natural surroundings have been respected.

The path back to the house leads past a huge, soft bed of lavender growing in such luxuriant profusion that one is tempted to dive right into it. But not before seeing the crowning jewel of the garden of Coltibuono: a strawberry tree (*Arbutus unedo*) around three hundred years old, with a trunk some 60 centimeters in diameter – a real museum piece of nature. It is also a rarity in this area and a living testimony to the attention and love that has been lavished on the plants of Coltibuono from the fifteenth century, the time of Abbot Francesco di Moncino, to the present day.

LA FERRIERA

*An oasis of greenery created out of
the arid soil of Pescia Fiorentina by Contessa
Giuppi Pietromarchi*

A country road through great expanses of ripe yellow wheat on the border between Tuscany and Lazio leads to a lush, green oasis, the garden of La Ferriera, which has been created by Contessa Giuppi Pietromarchi over the last twenty years.

It has required both vision and hard work in order to make this cool haven in the heat and blinding glare of the Maremma, a name that refers not merely to the coastal plains of southern Tuscany but to a large and poorly defined area that was once synonymous with marshland and malaria. A few measures had been taken by the former owners of this garden to protect it from the summer heat. They had planted four broad rows of pine trees right in front of

ABOVE: 'SOUVENIR DE ST ANNE' ROSES AND OLIVE TREES.
RIGHT: THE VIEW THROUGH THE UMBRELLA PINE-COVERED LAWN TO THE HOUSE.

the villa and, to its left, an olive grove. Thus an old garden did exist on this site, and it is on this foundation, without altering the original structure, that Giuppi Pietromarchi has laid out the splendid garden that can be seen there today. Olives, pines, and cypresses are an essential, indeed almost sacrosanct, feature of the Tuscan landscape and they have been treated as such by an artist and gardener who has set about making this garden her life's work.

The Maremma is a poor and arid region, where there is no tradition of gardening or the cultivation of flowers. Hence it was necessary to create a garden that has strong ties with the local vegetation and with the surrounding landscape. My friend's inspired creativity has succeeded in this superbly. Hers might be described as a country garden of a very special kind, in which rare and exotic plants are mingled with local ones without this resulting in any kind of clash; where purple and silver artichokes grow side by side with the extraordinary 'Papa Meilland' roses, and where *Salvia azurea* stands proudly in the midst of a sward of mint and basil.

Every time I visit La Ferriera I am first struck by the sight of the emerald-green lawn, firm but yielding, that covers the area underneath the umbrella pines (*Pinus pinea*) near the house. This lawn has cost years of continuous effort, for both the loamy nature of the soil and the acidity produced by the falling pine needles made it necessary to try out a variety of different seeds before coming up with a successful combination. The final result has been produced by the use of *Dichondra micrantha* (syn. *D. repens*), *Agrostis stolonifera* grass and a blend of seeds known as "Skia mix," specially made up for partially shaded situations. In the fall, the lawn is covered by a fine layer of dried cow manure mixed with peat; in the spring, on the other hand, a compost based on nitrates, phosphates, and potash (N.P.K.) is used. During the summer, a constant level of humidity is maintained by an automatic watering system that functions at night.

The pine wood covers a gently sloping area of about three hundred square meters: the luxuriant foliage of the

THE LAWN FROM THE HOUSE.

trees forms a sheltering green roof overhead and the lawn a green carpet beneath: there are no flowers here, for green alone holds sway. Giuppi Pietromarchi explains that it took her several years to reach this decision, after many attempts at creating areas of color. She believes that color should be used in blocks, as this creates an impression of greater space, and her garden is a fine demonstration of this principle.

The only flowering plants allowed here are to be found along the low wall that separates the pine wood from the olive grove: columbines, *Hydrangea quercifolia*, and *Viola cornuta* have sowed themselves naturally to form a narrow colored border along the edge of the lawn. The lawn itself is enclosed at the end by a wall one meter high that is completely covered with *Jasminum officinale*, and the wall is broken in the middle by a flight of three very broad stone steps, framed by two ancient Roman amphorae and two earthenware vases containing white petunias. At the sides of the steps, two pergolas built from chestnut poles support the jasmine, which is intertwined with the climbing rose 'New Dawn', while at the bottom of the right-hand side a hedge of 'Complicata' roses bursts into flower during the month of May. The area to the left is entirely covered by blue *Plumbago auriculata*. These steps lead to the "new garden", so-called

because in 1967 there was nothing here but a sheep pasture without a single tree. It is an almost circular area which today is planted up with an impressive display of trees and shrubs; they are grouped around a central lawn which shows their variety of form and color to advantage. To the right are specimens of mimosa (*Acacia dealbata*), golden wattle (*Acacia floribunda*), a pepper tree (*Schinus molle*), and *Clerodendrum fragrans*; nearby is a group of three large holm oaks, with a few Italian cypresses, and an area containing typically Mediterranean plants such as *Myrtus communis*, *Phillyrea angustifolia*, and Spanish broom (*Spartium junceum*). To the left, a few olive trees, a group of cork oaks, more holm oaks, and American red oaks form a small wood. Here the garden is entirely bounded by cypresses interspersed, every ten meters, with an umbrella pine; behind them, the harsh glare of the sun reflects off the surrounding countryside and the fields of grain.

Further up, towards the house, is the olive grove where Giuppi Pietromarchi has planted large bushes of old-fashioned roses in groups of three, creating highlights of color alongside the majestic, age-old shapes of the olive trees. The light that floods this part of the garden at dawn is refracted into a kaleidoscope of color, which mingles the silvery-white tones of the olives with the pale yellows, pinks, and soft whites of the roses. One of the first things one notices about La Ferriera is the extent to which the character of the surrounding landscape has been respected; luminous vistas open up between judiciously planted trees, and great care has been taken to avoid contrasts that are too violent. Harmonies of form and color are used to brilliant effect.

At the entrance to the olive grove is a rose-covered gazebo, where the predominant color is pink: from the very pale pink of 'Souvenir de la Malmaison', a Bourbon rose of 1843, to the 'Variegata di Bologna' with white and carmine stripes, another Bourbon variety from 1909, and the pinkish-white 'Souvenir de Saint Anne's'. A touch of brighter color is provided by the vivid yellow of 'Chinatown', which has an intense perfume, while the

A BOUGAINVILLEA-COVERED COTTAGE IN THE NEW GARDEN.

softer 'Felicia', a pale pink hybrid musk shaded with orange, is more delicate. Large clumps of the rosy white musk 'Penelope' light up the gray leaves of the olive trees, and, on the left, a flight of stone steps formed by festoons of the climber 'Alberic Barbier' and the Bourbon 'Boule de Neige' runs down to the lawn, its broad steps almost completely covered by 'Sea Foam'; underneath the roses are white, pale yellow, and blue specimens of bearded iris.

These roses have produced good results in the fairly temperate microclimate created by planting at La Ferriera. The excessive heat of August does slightly impede the growth of the plants, and occasional winter frosts have also determined the choice of species, which has naturally been made with local conditions in mind.

Along the left side of the house runs a terrace built of irregular pieces of local stone interplanted with *Dichondra micrantha*. The unifying element here is the five large olive trees surrounded by circular flowerbeds containing a delightful mixture of *Gardenia jasminoides*, (syn. *G. Grandiflora*), *Fuchsia magellanica*, bearded irises, *Bergenia crassifolia*, 'Penelope' and 'Unique Blanche' roses, and *Ceratostigma griffithii*. One bed is completely covered with *Hypericum* 'Hidcote', which form a yellow carpet in the month of June. The *Polygala myrtifolia* is in flower for practically ten months of the year and blends effectively with the splendid deep blue spikes of *Echium fastuosum* alongside it. No attempt has been made here to limit the color range; instead plants have been chosen to provide color throughout the summer months, when this terrace becomes the center of life at La Ferriera. A pergola of honeysuckle (*Lonicera caprifolium*) shelters this corner of the garden from the searing heat of summer. There is a single element of order and precision: four large earthen-ware vases, made by a Sicilian craftsman, overflow with white petunias. Another touch of white is provided by the *Datura ceratocaula*, whose calyces open at night to give off an intoxicating scent.

From the left of the terrace a path leads through the Blue Garden, where ancient olives overhang a slope covered with African lilies, *Agapanthus africanus*, *Hebe* 'Midsummer Beauty', *Duranta repens* (syn. *D. plumieri*), *Hibiscus syriacus* 'Blue Bird' and *Salvia azurea*, all of them blending into a strong blue haze beneath the silver leaves of the olives.

But the biggest surprise at La Ferriera for me is the small enclosure in which Giuppi has created a botanical garden with the plants brought back from her innumerable travels; for she is an inveterate plant collector. The *Hedychium gardnerianum* was brought from India, the large Jerusalem thorn (*Parkinsonia aculeata*) from South America, the coral tree (*Erythrina crista-galli*) from Brazil and the *Eupatorium atrorubens* from Mexico. This area is the product of a mind overflowing with imagination and enthusiasm, and it reflects the deep love and understanding that Giuppi Pietromarchi feels for her plants. She has shaped a garden that is a shining example of the human mind working in perfect harmony with nature.

AGAPANTHUS IN THE BLUE GARDEN.

LA FOCE

Where two valleys meet a bounty of wisteria and roses created by Marchesa Iris Origo

The landscape that I pass through on my way to the estate of La Foce in Val d'Orcia, located at the point where two valleys meet, always reminds me of the one depicted in Benozzo Gozzoli's fresco in the Medici-Riccardi chapel in Florence: steep hills, their flanks covered with tall and slender cypresses, form the backdrop to a light and airy landscape of broad horizons.

The owner of this garden was Marchesa Iris Origo, the daughter of a distinguished American diplomat, Bayard Cutting, whose parents, from an old New York family, had a splendid home in Westbrook, on the southern shore of Long Island. There they laid out a park of great beauty: the house was surrounded by tall oaks, and shrubs and ferns led down through woods

ABOVE: THE STONE FOUNTAIN IN THE MIDDLE OF THE CENTRAL CANAL IN THE FORMAL ITALIAN GARDEN. THE PERGOLA ALONG THE WALL IS COVERED BY 'MERMAID' ROSES.
LEFT: VIEW FROM THE HOUSE ACROSS THE STONE FOUNTAIN TOWARDS THE WALLED GARDEN.

THE STATUE OF A HERDSMAN AND BUFFALO WHICH HAS BEEN COVERED BY
IVY CONTAINED WITHIN A SMALL HEDGE OF BOX BY THE ENTRANCE TO THE HOUSE.

form that bare clay into fields of grain, to turn those mutilated woods green again, . . . that, we were sure, was the life we wanted."

It was here that Iris Origo, together with her husband Marchese Antonio Origo, was to create her garden. The task was entrusted to the English architect Cecil Pinsent who began the project in 1935. Pinsent was part of the Florentine intellectual circle that revolved around Bernard Berenson and his friends, and he worked in Florence from 1912 until 1938, restoring the gardens of I Tatti, where Berenson lived, of Villa Medici, the property of Lady Sybil Cuffe, where Iris Origo spent many years of her childhood, and of Le Balze, now owned by Georgetown University, where Pinsent designed the garden for C.A. Strong, who had married a daughter of John D. Rockefeller.

Originally the villa of La Foce was an old inn, dating from the sixteenth century, standing amidst arid hills completely bare of trees. For many years the total lack of water prevented the creation of a garden, but eventually a canal was dug, ten kilometers long, to bring water from a spring in the mountains; it made the realization of the long-desired garden a possibility at last. Designed in the classical Italian style on a number of different levels and terraces, the garden is separated from the road by a stone wall whose rigidity of line is softened by large ornamental vases placed at intervals to frame and enhance the views from this side of the property. A formal Italian garden was laid out at the back of the villa: a stone fountain supported by two dolphins stands in the middle of the central lawn, which is enclosed by flower beds containing a profusion of *Vinca major* and bordered with box; on the left, opposite the villa, a bower containing a stone bench and a table has been hollowed out of a large thicket of laurel. Parallel with one wall of the building runs a pergola completely covered in wisteria and 'Mermaid' roses. The predominant colors in this part of the garden are yellow and lilac, colors that reappear along a wall covered with clumps of aubretia and golden alyssum, while the lawn is bordered by irises and daffodils, with a

to three small lakes bordered by large thickets of azaleas and rhododendrons. In 1954, the park in Westbrook was opened to the public and transformed into a botanical garden. Marchesa Origo's mother was Lady Sybil Cuffe, the daughter of Lord Desart whose family seat, the country house of Desart Court in Ireland, was surrounded by a large garden in the Italian manner, filled with a great abundance of intermingled lilacs, laurels, hawthorns, and rhododendrons.

Iris Origo was the author of numerous works both in Italian, such as *Il mercante di Prato* (*The Merchant of Prato*) and *Bernardino da Siena e il suo tempo*, and in English, including *Allegra*, *The Last Attachment*, and *A Measure of Love*. In her book *Immagini e ombre* (*Images and Shadows*), she lovingly describes the atmosphere of La Foce:

". . . that vast, solitary, unspoilt landscape charmed and enthralled us: to live in the shadow of that mysterious mountain, to halt the erosion of those steep hills, to trans-

THE DRAMATIC LIGHT OF A STORM EMPHASIZES THE THEATRICAL SETTING OF THE LOWER GARDEN.

ABOVE: A BALUSTRADE LEADING TO THE BOX HEDGES OF
THE LOWER FORMAL GARDEN.
RIGHT: THE VIEW OVER THE LOWER FORMAL GARDEN WITH
BOX HEDGES AND MAGNOLIA GRANDIFLORA.

bed of yellow roses to one side. The whole of this area is sheltered and separated from the rest of the garden: a secluded place filled with flowers. Beyond it, an opening framed by two tall stone vases leads to a walled garden of clipped box hedges and squares of lawn, each square containing a lemon tree in a terracotta vase set on a stone base. Around the walls are *Clematis montana rubens*, *Philadelphus virginalis*, flowering pomegranates, white and violet *Hibiscus syriacus*, and a large number of tree and herbaceous peonies, roses and hydrangeas.

On the left, overlooking the valley, runs the pergola, which is one of the principal features of La Foce: it runs right through the garden to the foot of the hill, supporting an immense wisteria that makes a delightfully shady walkway and, in late spring, fills the garden with the delicate but intoxicating scent of its flowers.

A few steps lead to an upper level, where large beds of roses are clearly marked out by a stone border. The pergola extends the length of a small walk, the wisteria interspersed here with climbing roses; it leads to more flowerbeds containing tree peonies, *Hemerocallis*, and lavender. At this point, honeysuckle takes over from the wisteria and at the same time the garden changes in style: large bushes of weigela, *Forsythia* x *intermedia* 'Spectabilis', spiraea, *Rosa* 'Mutabilis', dog rose, and broom grow on the sides of the hill like wild plants. The scent of the flowers, the light filtering through the cypresses, and the fresh air of the wood turn this part of the garden into an oasis, where man has worked in perfect harmony with nature.

Descending again to the level of the villa, a stone path bordered by hedges of box is terminated by a balustrade overlooking the great valley; below lies yet another formal garden, ringed by tall cypresses, with a central axis that leads to a fountain in the middle and to a large stone bench that serves as a backdrop. Here too are flowerbeds surrounded by box, with a *Magnolia grandiflora* at the center. Through the screen of cypress trees can be glimpsed the magnificent panorama of the Val d'Orcia. The contrast between the garden and the natural countryside below it is almost unreal: the deep clay furrows follow one another like waves on the sea; in the background the burnt brown earth contrasts with rows of cypresses climbing uphill as if in procession. Turning back to the garden, it seems that its owners must have wanted to protect themselves from the power and desolation of the landscape around them, and to take refuge in the ordered formal structure of the classical Italian garden. A grotto with a fountain is hollowed out of the large wall that supports the terrace, and to the left of a flight of steps an *Acacia dealbata* softens the severity of the stonework.

Over the years, Marchesa Origo selected plants that stood up well to both the cold winters and the dry summers, as well as to the calcareous nature of the soil; here roses bloom profusely as do lavender, thyme, rosemary, and peonies. The jasmines, lemon trees, and fuchsias are moved to a large, unheated, south-facing greenhouse in the winter.

Another distinctive feature of the garden of La Foce is the fact that the Anglo-Saxon spirit of the owner clearly underlies the classical character of its traditional Italian design. Iris Origo complemented its formalism by her very careful selection of plants, set in extremely well-chosen locations. In the area facing the hillside, where there are no stone walls to keep nature at bay, the fantastic variety of forms and colors achieved solely by the skilful planting of flowering shrubs has created an enchanting and perfectly balanced pictorial scheme. Here, perhaps, Iris Origo wanted to create an effect that would recall the park in Westbrook that she knew as a child, just as in some way or other we all like to re-create our childhood memories.

Marchesa Origo is no longer alive, but the wisteria she planted at La Foce many years ago undoubtedly sprang from the seeds of her memories of the great park in Westbrook, Long Island, and the luxuriant garden of Desart Court, two places that marked and shaped her life and, as she recalls in her memoirs *Immagine e Ombre*, instilled in her her passion for gardens.

VILLADEATI CASTLE

*The literary retreat of Inge Feltrinelli in
the chalk hills of Monferrato*

The castle of Villadeati lies in the heart of the Monferrato district of Piedmont, to the east of Turin. An area of chalk hills spread out beneath a cold
transparent sky and defended by innumerable castles, it is also a land of
orchards and vineyards where the majority of the region's most celebrated
wines are produced.

Plantations of poplars, fields of rice and maize, and rows of willows follow
the course of the Stura stream beside the winding road that leads to Villadeati,
a picturesque village set on a hill overlooking the valley. Once known as
Corte de Scataldeis, it took its present name from the Deati family, who held
it in fief from the Visconti of Valenza. An ancient fort, which then stood on

ABOVE: LOOKING ACROSS THE SECOND GARDEN TOWARDS THE ARCADED GALLERY.
RIGHT: THE NEARBY TOWN OF VILLADEATI.

top of the hill, was destroyed in 1630 and, at the end of the eighteenth century, its place was taken by a romantic villa-castle, probably built to the design of Francesco Ottavio Magnocavallo; bristling with balustrades, loggias, and little towers, it dominates the village below. The castle and its surrounding buildings were bought in 1958 by Giangiacomo Feltrinelli, man of action, idealist, and founder of the famous Milanese publishing house that bears his name. He devoted many years of his short life not only to restoring the main house – consisting of a slender tower flanked by two lateral blocks and faced by a broad, raised courtyard – and the various outlying buildings scattered among graceful terraced gardens, but also to reviving the spirit of a place which, towards the end of the thirties, had been a focal point for writers.

His widow, Inge Feltrinelli, has kept faith with this spirit, bringing the original terraces back to life and laying out new ones that unite the natural slopes in a perfectly balanced harmony of color. The garden seems

ABOVE: ACROSS THE FRONT LAWN IN THE FIRST GARDEN.
LEFT: LATE NINETEENTH-CENTURY BUST AND MASSED FLOWERS ALONG THE WALL
OF THE SECOND GARDEN.

VILLADEATI CASTLE'S TERRACES FROM BELOW.

stone balustrade and columns faced with terracotta tiles. This is the true heart of Villadeati, an open-air drawing room decorated with bougainvilleas and lemon trees in pots. The extraordinary delicacy of the balustrade creates the illusion that the green of the grass continues uninterruptedly as far as the woods covering the distant hills, though it actually owes its magic to a highly sophisticated architectural device. From the center of this terrace runs an arcaded gallery about fifteen meters long, which leads to a small rotunda looking out over the boundless, gently rolling hills of the Monferrato. An internal staircase descends to the second garden, where an enormous wisteria covers the wall rising up to the balustrade; this terrace, also grass-covered, is smaller than the first and entirely surrounded by beds of brilliantly colored roses. Two palm trees (*Trachycarpus fortunei*) stand like sentinels on each side of the gallery, their plumes of foliage reaching up to the roof, and the tropical note is echoed by the *Yucca aloifolia* in the grass nearby. On the left is a large yew tree whose cool shade makes this second level seem more spacious than it is.

The approach to the third terrace is flanked symmetrically by two large clumps of *Hibiscus syriacus*, planted very close together in groups of three so that they form single masses of white flowers like a cloud, which last throughout the summer. Farther on, large specimens of lilac-colored *Buddleia davidii* and a wall covered with *Campsis radicans* mark the way to a large swimming pool on the right, exposed to the sun and sheltered from the wind by two huge trees, a cypress and a cedar of Lebanon, the sides of the pool are partially enclosed by *Hydrangea aspera villosa*, tree peonies, and roses, and its setting is superb: once in the water, one has the feeling of swimming among the clouds.

The fourth terrace is narrower than the others, but opens out onto the vineyard that slopes down the hillside from this level, like a natural extension of the garden. A small heated greenhouse built against the retaining wall of the terrace above is used to protect the lemon trees that ornament this area from winter frost.

almost to be suspended in the sky above the light mist that rises from the valley, creating a sense of detachment from reality that calls Magritte to my mind, or *A Midsummer Night's Dream*; it is a place for meditation and renewal, a piece of architectural fantasy set against the abstract geometry of the landscape.

The garden's seven terraces flow down toward the valley, linked together by small external and internal flights of steps. On the first terrace is a broad lawn enclosed by the two outer wings of the villa, and by a

Long beds filled with roses, *Hibiscus syriacus*, delphiniums, petunias, and zinnias make the fifth terrace a delightful mass of color, softly intermingled with the silver-gray of a few olive trees. At its center is a gigantic cedar of Lebanon, which rises to the height of the rotunda on the main terrace, its wide horizontal branches contrasting dramatically with the tall slender arcading of the gallery. Beyond the cedar are hydrangeas, peonies, phlox, and dahlias, stretching as far as a table enclosed by a small group of birches, reminiscent of a German or Austrian garden; Giangiacomo Feltrinelli may, it seems, have deliberately designed this area as a reminder of his childhood spent amid the woods of Styria. A tall cypress marks the beginning of a large terraced kitchen garden.

The sixth terrace is devoted to fruit trees, including pomegranates, and an artichoke bed; the only flowers are chrysanthemums. Neatly arranged and functional, this section is laid out on a gentle slope running down to the lowest level of the garden, which consists exclusively of vineyards and an orchard that blend naturally and easily into the landscape.

Imagination and method have been employed in equal measure at Villadeati to create a garden perfectly in tune with the architecture of the house and its charming

VINEYARDS BELOW THE FOURTH TERRACE.

ornamental buildings. It is a finely judged balancing act, subtle and impressive, decorative and disciplined at one and the same time, like the intricate pattern of vineyards that covers the undulating Monferrato landscape.

Together with her son Carlo, Inge Feltrinelli continues to improve her garden, adding continually to its delights and its display of summer color. And the castle of Villadeati is still a meeting point for writers and publishers, many of whom come together here to discuss future projects, and some perhaps even to be inspired with new ideas by the magic of this beautiful and remarkable garden in the hills of Monferrato.

ABOVE: THE ARCADED GALLERY AND THE MONFERRATO HILLS FROM THE TOP OF THE VILLA.
RIGHT: THE VIEW FROM THE FRUIT GARDEN'S ARCADES LOOKING DOWN ON TO THE GALLERY ROTUNDA.

LE FONTANELLE

The heritage of Magna Grecia fills the
terraces of Gianni Versace's classical garden
at Moltrasio on Lake Como

The heritage of Magna Grecia that Gianni Versace carries within him is apparent in the formal, classical character of his garden at Moltrasio, on Lake Como. One of its main sources of inspiration was Hadrian's Villa at Tivoli, whose theatrical architecture was surrounded by a garden that imitated the natural landscape, which in both Greece and Ancient Rome was considered the most appropriate setting for a place of worship.

Gianni Versace is the most internationally famous of Italian fashion designers: his first collection, "Donna", dates from 1978, when he also presented the Gianni Versace Uomo collection, and in 1983 and again in 1988 he won the "Cutty Sark", the highest American award for men's fashion. In

ABOVE: THE VILLA'S FAÇADE.
LEFT: LOOKING ACROSS THE FLORENTINE FLEURS-DE-LIS AND THE SHORE OF LAKE COMO.

1982 he had worked for the first time at La Scala, designing the costumes for Richard Strauss's ballet *Josephlegende*; this was the beginning of a long and unbroken collaboration through which over the years Versace has displayed the full range of his talents: he has designed costumes for many of Maurice Béjart's ballets as well as for operas directed by Bob Wilson, and he has collaborated with Roland Petit on a number of projects, designing costumes for Zizi Jeanmaire and Eric Vu An. His unceasing dedication to research, the innovative uses he has made of technology, and his ability to redefine taste in a fusion of fashion and theater design were all recognized when he received the Stanley Award, the highest mark of recognition in the fashion world.

Versace's fascination with the theater is reflected in his garden at Moltrasio. He acquired the property in 1978, and the garden together with its collection of eighteenth-century plants, was in a state of total neglect.

His passion for flowers and gardens was instilled in him by Sir Roy Strong, the landscapist and writer, who guided and inspired him in the work of laying out this great lakeside park.

A long, wide avenue, lined with sweet bay and cherry laurel and decorated with statues in niches, leads to the villa from the main road. In the broad curves traced out by this avenue are clumps of rhododendrons, azaleas, and hydrangeas, the flowers for which Lake Como is principally famous.

A dense green grove of palm trees (*Trachycarpus fortunei*) seem to have found their natural habitat here, spreading out alongside the villa and extending upwards into a wood of holm oaks, cypresses, Scots pines, and black spruce (*Picea mariana*). Close by is a small Italian-style garden, with a fountain and a pool at its center, filled with water arums and water lilies and surrounded by small white begonias and box. It is enclosed by a tall iron framework, surmounted by pyramids of stone, which serves as a support for a scented white wall of *Trachelospermum jasminoides*. A balustrade topped with stone baskets of fruit overlooks a larger Italian garden laid out below.

From this point, a small flight of steps descends to the entrance to the great landscaped park that stretches as far as the shore of the lake, where huge plane trees trail their branches in the water. Majestic cypresses and holly trees are interspersed with camellias and underplanted with a carpet of *Pachysandra terminalis*, which thrives on shade and damp, encircled by a border of lilyturf (*Ophiopogon japonicus*).

A gravel path leads to the walk along the lake side, with a belt of red impatiens bordered once again by lilyturf. The paths here are ornamented with stone vases in the eighteenth-century style, from which pink geraniums cascade over ivy-covered pillars, while other vases hold box plants pruned into the shape of balls. The trees – planes, lindens, cedars of Lebanon, and Scots pines – have been planted with sufficient space between them to allow them to spread their branches freely and to be seen clearly in silhouette. A bed of lilac and pink azaleas to the left follows the undulating contours of the ground gently downwards, extending as far as an enormous clump of *Fibigia clypeata*, aspidistra, and *Pachysandra terminalis*; a little further on a group of hydrangeas and spireas form a circle beneath a group of beeches. The path emerges from the shade into a large area of lawn flanked by a long border of 'Queen Elizabeth' roses. The small greenhouse here is used to shelter the lemon trees in winter and to cultivate seedlings in spring; in front of it stretches an expanse of pink roses, which opens onto a basin framed by stone statues draped with ivy. On the terrace that covers this basin is a solarium surrounded by potted oleanders and azaleas. A fine staircase leads down to the lake, where boats are moored; and a path leads uphill to a long walk through the wood.

From the edge of the lake the villa is concealed from view by a tall *Pittosporum tobira*, a large magnolia, and a magnificent holly: cast-iron tables and chairs are set out in the shade of the trees for idyllic summer lunches. The larger of the two Italian-style gardens, with its two vast flowerbeds bordered with box, is impressive from this vantage point: two elegant Florentine fleurs-de-lis are

A VIEW OF THE SMALL ITALIAN-STYLE GARDEN FROM ONE OF THE CLIFF PATHS.

VASES OF GERANIUMS ALONG THE LAKESIDE.

outlined in red begonias against the emerald green backdrop of the lawn, and the design is highlighted still further by an edging of white gravel. The stone vases containing lemon trees and box are a traditional feature of the formal Italian garden. At the center is a circular basin with arum lilies (*Zantedeschia aethiopica*) and water lilies, in line with the flight of steps leading down to the lake; eighteenth-century style vases with red and pink geraniums add a striking flourish to the parapet. The façade of the villa is decorated by a double staircase completely covered with *Trachelospermum jasminoides*.

The landscaped park resumes, on the other side of the villa, with a large expanse of lilyturf enclosed by a screen of strawberry trees (*Arbutus unedo*) that have grown to a remarkable size. Large groups of European fan palms (*Chamaerops humilis*) and clumps of *Spiraea x vanhouttei* introduce a new note to the landscape: the narrow path continues along the water's edge, past yews and an enormous linden tree, to end at a small rotunda with an unforgettable view of Lake Como. The hydrangeas, bay trees, and yews, and the small roses that climb the railings here intensify the romantic atmosphere of a spot from which it is always hard to tear myself away.

On the entrance level is a third Italian-style garden:

THE LAKESIDE PATH.

almost identical to the first, it repeats, on a smaller scale, the design of the main one in front of the villa. The impressive barrier of naturalized palm trees marks the end of the garden at this point, and again steep paths lead up to a walk through the wood that borders the whole upper part of the property.

Abandoned for about fifty years, the garden has been restructured on the basis of a study of old designs that reflect the taste of the late eighteenth and early nineteenth centuries. Landscape gardener Pier Luigi Ratti helped Versace to carry out the work with great care and respect for the local flora, always keeping in mind the character of the surrounding landscape and the traditional style of the gardens of Lake Como: the mildness of the climate allows not only conifers to thrive here but also Mediterranean species, such as the olive, and exotic and tropical plants. At the height of the flowering season it is the rhododendrons and azaleas that represent the main attraction of the great gardens of Lake Como.

Gianni Versace's aim was to bring an old garden back to life, and he has fully succeeded in this, brilliantly resurrecting Le Fontanelle and filling it with his own spirit so that it mirrors perfectly both his sense of classical discipline and his deep sense of theater.

BOTTOM: VIEW FROM THE BOAT HOUSE.
TOP: THE CLASSICAL DESIGNS OF THE BALUSTRADE WHICH CONTAIN
ONE OF THE ITALIAN GARDENS AT THE FOOT OF THE ROCKY CLIFF WALL.
RIGHT: 'QUEEN ELIZABETH' ROSES FLANKING THE LAKESIDE LAWN
AND THE BOAT MOORINGS.

VILLA FOGAZZARO

*Three terraces of exquisite delicacy
for the great grandson of a great writer,
Marchese Giuseppe Roi*

Almost on the border with Switzerland, on the eastern branch of Lake Lugano, is the small village of Oria; it lies right on the shoreline, south of the Valsolda, and whenever I go there, Villa Fogazzaro appears to me to be rising straight out of the water. Built in the nineteenth century, it was the home of the writer and poet Antonio Fogazzaro, and the inspiration for his famous novel *Piccolo mondo antico*.

"Amidst all the fluctuating light and shade brought by the sun to the mountains and lake, one thing does not vary, the joyful expression with which the guest is always welcomed here." These words are written on the inside of the door of one of the guest rooms, signed by the composer Zanella

ABOVE: THE SMALL TERRAZZA AT THE SIDE OF THE HOUSE.
LEFT: THE STEPS LEADING TO THE HOUSE WITH TERRACOTTA POTS FILLED WITH MARIGOLDS.

THE PLAQUE TO ANTONIO FOGAZZARO, POET AND GREAT-GRANDFATHER
OF MARCHESE GIUSEPPE ROI.

the mildness of the climate, faces out over the water. Against the house is an *Osmanthus fragrans*, which fills the air with an intense perfume in spring and fall. Like everything else in this garden, which has remained intact ever since its creation, these are all typically nineteenth-century plants. The house is bordered all the way round by *Ceratostigma plumbaginoides*, the vivid blue flowers throwing the white blooms of the roses into relief.

Two flights of steps, decorated with terracotta vases of geraniums, lead to the second level, where the retaining wall is again covered with *Ficus pumila* and *Trachelospermum jasminoides*. Here there are two small beds of red begonias bordered with box, a large cypress supporting a *Jasminum officinale affine*, and yet another *Osmanthus fragrans*. Another staircase descends from the middle of the terrace, its sides completely covered with *Trachelospermum jasmsinoides*, whose glossy dark green leaves set off the beautiful terracotta vases overflowing with yellow marigolds that garland the steps. At the sides stand two pale pink *Lagerstroemia indica*.

Pink gravel sets the third terrace apart from the others. In the center is another palm, surrounded by a carpet of *Dichondra micrantha* and red begonias bordered with box, and at the sides are four cypresses. A group of lemon trees has been planted at the base of the wall, which is covered with 'Albéric Barbier' roses, a wonderfully romantic variety that was much in vogue in Italy in the early years of this century. Ivy and winter jasmine (*Jasminum nudiflorum*), which has a mass of tiny yellow flowers in the dark days of winter, grow along the wall that encloses the property. The whole façade of the house on this side is buried under an immense wisteria that runs along the balustrade and climbs up to the fourth floor.

Looking out over the railing that separates the garden from the water lapping almost at its edge, and contemplating the mountains that roll like waves into the lake, I always feel myself steeped in the atmosphere of the nineteenth century: the violets, roses, palms, wisteria, and *Osmanthus fragrans* are themselves part of the exquisite, sweet-scented natural world which provided

and dated 1865. The same cordiality and hospitality is still practised today by Marchese Giuseppe Roi, great grandson of the writer, and his enchanting house still welcomes visitors as if time had not moved on.

To reach the villa from the main road, a steep, covered staircase leads down to the second floor of the house, where the drawing room opens onto the small garden; there a succession of three terraces, covering an area only ten meters wide and twenty meters long, slopes down to the level of the water. It is a tiny, exquisitely delicate garden, decorated as if it were itself a drawing room and I love to relax, dream or read there in the mild summer afternoons. The palms, the lemon trees, the *Osmanthus fragrans*, and the cypresses are the walls of the room; the flower beds are the carpets on the floor; the climbing roses and jasmines, the flower-patterned coverings; and the terracotta vases filled with geraniums and little red begonias are the *objets d'art*.

On the first terrace the walls are covered with white climbing roses, and the parapet overlooking the lake is completely overgrown with *Ficus pumila*; two splendid lemon trees in large terracotta vases frame the view, and a tall, slender palm (*Trachycarpus fortunei*), a reminder of

THE THIRD TERRACE FROM THE SMALL BALUSTRADE. GERANIUMS AND MARIGOLDS OVERWHELM THE EYE.

the source of inspiration for so many of the most famous poems of the last century.

Là, tout n'est qu'ordre et beauté,
Luxe, calme et volupté.

This garden could well adopt Baudelaire's verses as its motto, for what is most striking here is the sense of order with which the plants, vases, flower beds and steps are all arranged, the concentrated spaces of the terraces perfectly contrasting the majesty of the surrounding landscape.

To the west of the house lies the small square terrace known as "la terrazza della lirica" (the terrace of lyric poetry), enclosed by a cupola of *Rosa banksiae*. From

there there is a charming view of a long pergola covered in wisteria, ivy, and Virginia creeper (*Parthenocissus quinquefolia*), of terracotta vases containing *Acalypha wilkesiana*, and the vegetable garden. Typically Mediterranean shrubs such as broom, laurustinus (*Viburnum tinus*), rosemary, and sweet bay encircle a centuries-old pine tree that frames the horizon, while oleanders and bay trees line the water's edge at its foot.

The characters of Fogazzaro's novels seem to belong here still, in this enchanting lakeside setting, and to have left a flavor of their presence behind in the atmosphere that permeates the garden to this day.

THE GARDEN'S EDGE AND LAKE LUGANO.

VILLA HRUSKA

*An Alpine landscape of rocks and
rivulets created by botanist Professor
Arturo Hruska on Lake Garda*

The microclimate, the quality of the light and the blue of the water make Lake Garda the most Mediterranean of the north Italian lakes, and Gardone Riviera, on its north-western shore, looking across the water to the majestic Monte Baldo, is a unique and remarkably beautiful garden. Here, within the space of only 10,000 square meters, can be found a range of plants from five continents, together with an Alpine garden that is one of the most comprehensive to be seen anywhere. Its creator, Professor Arturo Hruska, deeply moved by the beauty of the lake and drawn to the area because of the mildness of its climate, decided to buy a plot of land there in 1914. The young doctor, dentist, and botanist, descended from a Moravian noble family, had

ABOVE: THE DENSE BAMBOO FOLIAGE OF THE INDIAN GARDEN.
RIGHT: VIEW FROM THE TOP OF THE ALPINE GARDEN.

THE LITTLE BRIDGES POOL OF THE JAPANESE GARDEN.

attended several European universities, had traveled and studied in the United States, and had been appointed dental surgeon to the court of St Petersburg by Tsar Nicholas II. He undoubtedly belonged to that group of northern and central European intellectuals who found their way to Italy at the beginning of the century and remained there, dazzled by the beauty of the country. His plot of land, then a rustic vineyard on the slopes of Monte Lavino, which overlooks the lake, was bought piecemeal from a number of different farmers. As a naturalist and a great lover of the mountains, he wanted as far as possible to create an Alpine landscape of rocks, rivulets, and streams, in which the flora of the Dolomites could flourish. The greatest difficulty to be overcome at the beginning was that of raising the humidity level as the air of Lake Garda is generally dry and in summer very hot.

He first dug a canal to bring water to the site from a spring on the mountainside, and then devoted much careful thought to the planning of a rock garden; using dolomitic stones, he built a sort of rocky crag, about ten meters high, at the center of his plot of land, and around this nucleus laid out pools and streams. By skillful planting of conifers and rhododendrons, and thickets of bamboo, he introduced an endless variety of views, and with a screen of trees all round the property he concealed the nearby houses, creating the impression that the garden was an extension of the mountain slope.

A small path leads to the first section, the "English-style garden", whose name may derive from the fine lawn that runs right up to the house. It is surrounded by sub-tropical vegetation consisting of plants such as *Agave striata*, *Agave americana*, mimosa (*Acacia dealbata*), *Iochroma cyaneum*, India rubber plant (*Ficus elastica*), *Trachycarpus fortunei*, and *Hedychium coronarium*. A little brook runs beside the path to a pond spanned by a light bridge, from which falls a cascade of *Rosa banksiae lutea*; this is the "Japanese Garden", with its plantain trees (*Musa* x *paradisiaca*), large royal ferns (*Osmunda regalis*), *Colocasia esculenta*, maples, arum lilies, and *Begonia grandis*.

Further up is the "Indian Garden", which consists of a small grove of bamboo (*Phyllostachys viridis* and *P. heterocycla*) so dense that when I visit, I often lose my bearings. The sense of disorientation is only reinforced when one emerges from this tropical jungle to find oneself facing an Alpine valley, with pines and firs standing statuesquely against the pinnacles of the Dolomites. This is the "Alpine garden", where hundreds of typical Alpine species have found an ideal habitat among the artificial rocks laid out in imitation of the strange small peaks of Lavaredo and Il Sassolungo. The special feature of these rocks is that each block is built out of a core of porous tufa covered with red Verona stone, with spaces and cracks left so that the roots of the plants can penetrate into the damp tufa, finding the humidity and coolness they require. Drainage canals, dug between one block and the next, prevent the water from stagnating. The effect is extraordinary, especially in spring when clumps of heather, Alpine rhododendrons, gentians, saxifrages, primroses, and bellflowers transform these rocks into

flowered cushions set one on top of another. Little cascades of water fall from various heights to form tiny lakes, which help to maintain the humidity vital to these plants if they are to survive in a climate so different from their natural one. Such an enormous range of alpine and rock plants gathered in such a small space is a rare and spectacular sight: they come from all over the world and were collected by Professor Hruska either in the course of his innumerable travels or through exchanges with various international botanical gardens.

The highest part of the garden has been turned into a tropical area watered by a flower-bordered stream, which

THE 'DOLOMITIC' ROCK, WITH RED PINES GROWING FROM THE CRACKS.

runs across the middle of the lawn against a backdrop of *Agave americana*, *Yucca aloifolia* 'Variegata', *Chamaerops humilis*, and *Cycas revoluta*. Enclosing this level at the top are the greenhouses, and a small nursery for propagation, which have been looked after for over forty years by the gardener, Angiolino Amati, with the help of his wife and two children. Trained by Professor Hruska, he is an expert gardener who has kept alive the passion for plants handed down to him by his great teacher.

The garden is a marvelous synthesis of nature and

esthetics, producing an unending succession of color and variety throughout the year. It is unquestionably a reflection of the eclectic taste of the twenties and thirties, with its love for the exotic and remote, but above all it is a testament to a man with an abiding passion for the plants of the Dolomites. In 1954, Professor Hruska was invited to London to deliver a lecture at the Royal Horticultural Society on the ingenious methods he had employed in raising alpine plants in the subtropical climate of Lake Garda. His presence still seems to fill the garden he created and one would not be surprised today to turn a corner and catch a glimpse of him bent over his flowers. The personality of this great botanist and naturalist seems to be stamped indelibly on the place to which he gave so much of himself, though now that it has matured and taken on a shape of its own it is surely more magnificent than even he can have predicted at the beginning of his labors all those years ago in 1914.

ABOVE: ASTILBE VARIETIES ALONG THE STREAM EDGE.
TOP LEFT: BIRD'S NEST FERNS AND BEGONIA PANICLES GROWING SIDE BY SIDE.
LEFT: AGAVE AMERICANA IN THE TROPICAL AREA OF THE GARDEN.

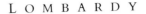

VILLA BAGATTI VALSECCHI

*In the family tradition Barone Pier Fausto
Bagatti Valsecchi suspends a patchwork of colors
in the mists of a lake*

The spell woven by the enchanting atmosphere of the lakes of Lombardy is to me subtle and irresistible. I love Como, in particular, with its temperate climate and Mediterranean vegetation, its splendid villas, and its high mountains plunging sheer into the water to enclose the three branches of the lake. It has some of the most impressive scenery to be found anywhere in Italy.

The road that leads from Menaggio to Valsolda, in the province of Como, climbs to a height of about four hundred meters, to the village of Grandola e Uniti, where a small group of stone houses with simply decorated façades clusters around a square that is a jewel of architectural simplicity. On its north side stands the Villa Bagatti Valsecchi, a wrought-iron gate, supported by

ABOVE: CASCADES OF PINK GERANIUMS TUMBLING FROM THE HOUSE ENTRANCE.
LEFT: THE ROCK GARDEN WITH THE NEW GARDENS ABOVE AS SEEN FROM THE PORTICO.

GERANIUMS AND IVY FRAME A SMALL STATUE IN THE
ENTRANCE COURTYARD.
RIGHT: VERBENIAS, ALYSSUM, 'BASKET-OF-GOLD' MARIGOLDS, AND CERATOSTIGMA
GROWING IN CRACKS IN THE COURTYARD'S STONE PAVING.

stone pillars topped with pyramids, marking the entrance to a small courtyard. Petunias, 'Basket-of-Gold' (*Alyssum saxatile*), marigolds, and bellflowers grow in the gaps in its stone paving, making a delicate patchwork that brightens the sober gray of the flagstones. Beneath the three orders of arches that frame the windows, which are ornamented with geometric motifs, cascades of pale pink geraniums offer an invitation to climb a long, narrow staircase open to the sky: at the top is a hanging garden built on rocks that overhang a gorge about five hundred meters deep, at the bottom of which flows the river Sanagra. Only a truly romantic and courageous mind could have conceived so imaginative a garden, amidst scenery reminiscent of the landscapes described by Charlotte Brontë in *Wuthering Heights*.

At the beginning of this century, Barone Pasino Bagatti Valsecchi, president at that time of the Società Orticola Lombarda (Lombard Horticultural Society), decided to transform his property into what is now the most spectacular rock garden anywhere in Italy. The work was continued by his son Pier Fausto, an architect,

and his daughter-in-law, who devoted much of their time to its care and development, as well as designing a new, modern garden to the left of the villa.

An architectural balancing act had been necessary to marry up the façade of the house looking onto the square with the much lower face overlooking the precipice in front of the house, and the difference in levels forms the basis for the design of the garden, which merges without interruption into the coniferous woodland of the natural landscape surrounding it.

THE EAST-FACING SIDE OF THE HOUSE AND PORTICO.

A long, narrow stretch of level ground in front of the house, enclosed by an iron balustrade, leads to a gentle downward slope where various types of conifer, plane trees, a large cedar of Lebanon, maples, rhododendrons, and ferns planted by Barone Pasino Bagatti Valsecchi, make a true collector's garden. The balustrade overlooks the rock garden, in which each winding ravine has been filled with plants well suited to the local conditions, such as the dwarf Hinoki cypress (*Chamaecyparis obtusa* 'Nana'), *Chamaecyparis Obtusa* 'Crippsii', *Juniperus*

horizontalis, *Picea abies* 'Repens', mountain pine (*Pinus mugo*), many different kinds of cotoneaster, and a variety of *Pyracantha coccinea*. Intrepid mountaineering gardeners have regularly to lower themselves on ropes to attend to the needs of the plants, whose contrasting colors make the sheer rock face an even more dramatic sight. From the front of the house the view is impressive: on one side of the gorge is the natural woodland garden, on the other the one laid out by man in imitation of nature.

Under the portico that runs along one side of the villa is a small gateway like the entrance to a *hortus conclusus*. It opens onto the new garden created by Pier Fausto, which is laid out on three terraces. Green lawns, endless vistas of flowers, wide open spaces, and gently sloping flights of steps greet the eye, offering a surprising and delightfully peaceful contrast to the precipice below.

The first large expanse of lawn is entirely surrounded by mixed borders filled with annual and perennial plants such as marigolds, petunias, lavender, fuchsias, cinerarias, verbenas, phlox, asters, and dahlias. The bright colors wind like a multicolored ribbon along the edge of the lawn and around the tall dark spires of a group of cypresses on the edge of the precipice. A balustrade runs along the edge of this first terrace, separating it from the gorge.

A few stone steps lead up to the second terrace, smaller than the first, where again a lawn provides a setting for flowers such as iris, rudbeckia, gaillardia, cosmos, and gazania. The gray stone retaining wall has itself become a miniature botanical garden, with a different plant between each of the stones, among them *Alyssum saxatile*, *Ceratostigma willmottianum*, wall pepper (*Sedum acre*), and *Saxifraga* × *arendsii*.

The third level is reached by means of another stone staircase whose steps are covered with prostrate creepers and small alpine plants, and the air fills with the scent of thyme as it is trodden underfoot. A fence runs along the side of the steps as far as three imposing cypresses which act as a focal point and a link between the different levels of the garden. The broad lawn is enclosed by a hedge of

A WINDING PATH AND THE ROCK GARDEN WHICH RUNS ALONG THE TOP OF THE RAVINE.

cherry laurel which in turn protects the wide mixed border. From this height the view of the mountains, woods, and gorge is incomparable; the sound of the river rises from the valley below, and the effect of the superb natural scenery is brilliantly enhanced by skilful planting throughout the garden.

Whenever I visit the Villa Bagatti Valsecchi I have no doubt as to just what a passion for gardening can mean: it would be hard to find a more challenging and unusual site than this one, where the natural landscape has been turned to extraordinary advantage in creating a garden that seems suspended amidst the mountains, perfectly combining the two principal elements of garden design, harmony and surprise, to magical effect.

Nature has been controlled, but no attempt has been made to impose upon the landscape anything out of sympathy with its own character: its identity has merely been more sharply defined by the grace and imagination of the planting scheme: the most striking example of this is the sheer rock face of the gorge, where the plants seem to be in their element, as if they have always been part of the magnificent landscape around them.

BOTTOM: VARIOUS CONIFERS ARE GROUPED TOGETHER FOR SHAPE AND COLOR
AND TO DRAMATIZE THE VIEW ACROSS THE RAVINE.
TOP: MIXED BORDERS OF ANNUALS AND PERENNIALS SURROUNDING THE FRUIT LAWN.
LEFT: THE THIRD LEVEL OF THE NEW GARDEN LEADING UP TO THE
CYPRESSES WHICH ACT AS A FOCAL POINT AND LINK BETWEEN THE DIFFERENT
LEVELS OF THE GARDEN.

VILLA CODROIPO BADOGLIO

In a region imbued with history and legend the magical aquatic garden of Duchessa Giuliana Badoglio Rota

Friuli-Venezia Giulia is a region that is perhaps not as well known as it deserves to be: its magnificent stretches of green countryside, vine-covered hills, and ancient houses, its troubled history, its legends, and the proud character of its people, make it one of the most interesting areas in the north of Italy.

To the north-east of Rivignano, the road leading to Udine runs for part of its length alongside the river Stella, which flows through the property of the dukes of Badoglio. On their estate stands the ancient villa that was once part of the fief of Flambruzzo, donated by Conte di Gorizia to the counts of Codroipo in 1466. The villa remained in the hands of the same family until

ABOVE: THE VILLA AND ITS REFLECTION IN THE RIVER STELLA.
RIGHT: A STYLIZED WOODEN BRIDGE WHICH JOINS THE TWO MAIN PARTS OF THE GARDEN.

THE SUN REFLECTED IN A SEA OF WATERLILIES.

the beginning of the century, when it was bought by Duca Badoglio.

A bridge over the Stella provides access to the villa, leading to a huge L-shaped piazza enclosed by the walls of the building. It is surrounded by a charming balcony adorned with red roses and a profusion of snapdragons. The garden proper extends from the grand terrace of the villa, with a vast lawn stretching away for about three hundred meters, framed by a majestic stand of oaks, sequoias, planes, holm oaks, and horse chestnuts, and dotted with small, brightly-colored islands of roses. One is immediately struck by the extraordinary peace that reigns here.

The garden has been designed and created around the river, with water playing the leading role and the trees providing the stage setting. The soil is alluvial and abounds with springs; one has only to dig down to the depth of a meter to reach the water table. The Stella branches repeatedly as it winds its way between the trees to form small green islands connected by slender bridges.

THE DIVERTED PART OF THE RIVER WITH ALDERS PREDOMINATING.

This is the realm of the swamp cypresses (*Taxodium distichum*), the dominant feature of the garden, which grow straight out of the water here as they do in their natural habitat. In some places they have also been planted along the river banks to consolidate the ground.

Close to the steps of the terrace, which are bordered at the base by a hedge of hydrangeas, are three unique specimens of *Osmanthus fragrans*: these trees, which normally grow to a height of about three meters, have attained an extraordinary size here, making them a botanical rarity.

The sweet scent given off by their flowers pervades the whole garden and contributes to the magical atmosphere created by the sight and sound of running water.

A little wooden bridge on the right-hand side of the park crosses the river, which has been dammed at this point to form a small lake. Above it stands a mound completely covered with periwinkle, which in spring turns into a mass of violet that is reflected in the water shimmering below.

The Stella runs through a wood of large oaks, planes,

and poplars, the banks of the river lined with indigenous aquatic plants. Every so often the long branches of *Lespedeza Thunbergii* add a note of color to the unbroken expanse of green with their small purple flowers. The river marks the boundary of the estate on the right-hand side of the wood.

From the bottom of the garden, the view back towards the villa seems to me magically serene: the majestic trees appear to float on the water like the masts of ghostly ships, framing the sky with their foliage. They have been skillfully planted to achieve a contrast of sunlight and deep shade, and the swamp cypresses cast their long shadows over the water: there is nothing more moving, as the Duc d'Harcourt once wrote, than seeing the last rays of the sun penetrate beneath their branches and set the red trunks of the trees on fire.

Duchessa Giuliana Badoglio, the architect of this delightful garden, has used plants to stimulate each of the five senses: that of smell with the scent of the *Osmanthus fragrans*, which grow right in front of the house, weaving a spell of such subtlety that it calls to mind the words of Théophile Gautier in *La Marguerite*, "la vue et le parfum de ces fleurs favorites. . . ."; that of sight with the continual play of light reflected in the water, and with single splashes of color – the hill of periwinkles or the pale hues of the roses – that bring the whole garden to life; that of sound with the flowing river – its subdued and gentle ripple growing louder where the water pours out from underneath the villa – and with the song of the birds that thrive in the shelter and luxuriance they find here; that of touch with the delight that comes from walking over the vast level expanse of velvety grass and reaching out to feel the different textures of leaves and flowers; and finally that of taste, with the fruit produced by the trees. It is a floating, dream-like garden, where scents, colors, and sounds all blend together in an atmosphere of almost supernatural tranquillity.

SPOTS OF COLOR LEAD TO A MOUND OF <u>ACER</u> <u>PALMATUM</u> <u>ATROPURPUREUM</u>.

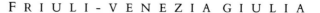

DUINO CASTLE

*The gardens of Principe Carlo della
Torre e Tasso descend in terraces to the
shores of Trieste*

Against an impressive background of rocks rising sheer out of the sea, Duino
Castle stands in the midst of the dense Mediterranean maquis, its massive
walls softened by a profusion of plants and trees. It was built on a site where,
according to legend, the Druids performed the rituals of moon worship in
Celtic times. A tower, which once formed part of a Roman outpost, still
stands intact after almost two thousand years: set in the wall is a memorial
tablet dedicated to Diocletian, who stayed there in the third century A.D.

In 1139, Duino was the fief of the Patriarch of Aquileia, and it was toward
the end of the thirteenth century that the della Torre family arrived in the
area. Numbering among their forebears Consuls, Captains, and Imperial

ABOVE: STATUES FLANK THE SEA-WARD SIDE OF THE MAIN CASTLE ENTRANCE.
LEFT: THE CASTLE AND WOODS FROM THE GARDEN'S LOWEST TERRACE.

Vicars of Milan and Lombardy, they extended their powers to become Princes and Sovereign Lords of Milan. Enlightened legislators, they were responsible for setting up the land register and the postal service, and for reconstructing the city after its invasion by Barbarossa. Defeated by their rivals, the Visconti family, they moved to Friuli, which saw a succession of four Torriani patriarchs in the fourteenth century. Dante Alighieri was a guest of Patriarch Pagano at the fief of Duino, where people still point out "Dante's Rock".

The della Torre were not just benefactors and promoters of public works but also *condottieri* in the endless

THE IVY HEDGE SURROUNDING THE MOAT.

wars against the Turks, and skillful diplomats throughout Friuli's complicated history. The influence of humanism, coupled with the family's traditional hospitality, made Duino a focal point in the nineteenth century for composers such as Franz Liszt and Johann Strauss, members of ruling dynasties, such as the Duchesse de Berry and Empress Elizabeth of Austria, writers such as Mark Twain, Paul Valery, and Gabriele D'Annunzio, and poets such as Hugo von Hofmannsthal and Rainer Maria Rilke. The latter, in particular, a close friend of Princess Marie von Höhenlohe-Thurn und Taxis, who inherited the castle, composed his appropriately named *Duino Elegies* here at Duino Castle in 1912.

In 1954, Principe Raimondo, the nephew of Princess Marie, eager to keep alive the cultural traditions of Duino, became one of the promoters and founders of the Center of Theoretical Physics at Miramare; in 1972, he set up the International Federation of Institutes for Advanced Studies and a Center for Studies of Rainer Maria Rilke. Another cultural project that emerged out of a collaboration between England and Duino was the *Collegio del mondo unito dell'Adriatico*, with Lord Louis Mountbatten and Principe Raimondo as its patrons. Today his son, Principe Carlo Alessandro, continues the work begun by his father, organizing international conventions and meetings on cultural and scientific topics.

But as well as being an enlightened and cultured man, Principe Raimondo was a great gardener: it was he who conceived the design of the splendid park at Duino and was responsible for its realization. In 1956, the garden was laid out around the castle on a series of terraces descending to the shoreline where a thick wood of holm oaks, cypresses, and laurels shelters it from the wind and the salt off the sea. In this north-eastern corner of Italy the wind known as the *bora* blows with astonishing force and violence, and it has been necessary at Duino to take full advantage of the protection offered by the castle walls.

A tall arch in the outer wall of the castle, entirely covered with *Parthenocissus tricuspidata* 'Veitchii', leads through to the moat, once filled with water but now transformed into a garden filled with flowers and carpeted with grass, bordered at the edges with beds of hydrangeas, daisies, sage, and impatiens, planted with no particular concern to create a restricted color range. This area is especially well protected by the high walls, and the plants grow riotously. To the right a swimming pool has been built in an open area beneath the walls, which are covered here with *Bignonia capreolata*. A large flower bed in the shape of a horseshoe spills over with roses in a multitude of colors, which grow healthy and strong here and provide flowers from May to October.

From this level, flights of stone steps descend to a second garden, whose perimeter wall is covered with ivy

THE SUNKEN SWIMMING POOL AND LAWN THROUGH THE ELABORATE GARDEN GATE.

mixed with blue clumps of *Ceratostigma plumbaginoides* and red valerian (*Centranthus ruber*). The combination is unusual but very effective as these plants, which grow well in the chinks between stones, have found an environment here that suits them perfectly. This area is about twenty meters long and six meters wide, with a little graveled path bordered by two beds of *Salvia splendens* on the right and a low retaining wall covered with pink and white geraniums and ageratum on the left; above, the trees of the Mediterranean maquis form a spectacular green wall. The path leads to a rotunda overlooking the sea, with a view of the small bay beneath

and of the great wood that stretches as far as Duino's private beach where I specially like to swim in summertime. Down a few more steps are some splendid specimens of yew, pruned into the shape of pyramids, that frame the sea in the background. In this garden I particularly love a tunnel of 'Clair Matin' roses opening to the right, supported by iron arches on a wall covered with *Viburnum tinus* and lined at the base with *Ceratostigma plumbaginoides*. Beside a strip of lawn to the left, there are large shrubs of *Hibiscus syriacus* which flower right through the summer.

This garden is made distinctive by its arrangement of

terraces, which are connected by a planting scheme that creates a sense of visual continuity and avoids any hint of discordance. Long avenues of cypresses are the unifying element, providing rhythmic links between the various levels of the garden; it is clear that great skill and care have been brought to bear in coordinating and integrating this complex design.

As it descends, the garden takes on the appearance of a park, broadening out into a large expanse of grass enclosed by cypresses and magnolias, with flower beds filled with megaseas (*Bergenia crassifolia*), gazanias, fuchsias, begonias, marigolds, and *Justicia rizzinii*.

Another path leads to the old ruined fortress, traditionally linked to the cult of the sun god and known by the romantic name of the "Dama Bianca" (the "White Lady"). Mediterranean plants such as oleanders, tamarisks, buddleia, viburnums, and laurels flank this delightful walk, which opens onto a small terrace – in my opinion the most spectacular point in the garden. It looks out across the sea, over the tops of the cypresses, and down onto the dense wood around the ancient ruins, and sweeps down to the rocks and the Adriatic below.

A long avenue of cypresses, carpeted with white, red, and pink impatiens, leads back to the castle, and a second avenue, again of cypresses, makes an imposing frame for an ancient Roman statue. The garden has been designed for peaceful walks, with resting places at intervals from which to admire the dramatically beautiful scenery.

The last point on this tour of Duino is an area set aside for the cultivation of flowers for cutting; in a small greenhouse, Nino, the gardener here since 1956, raises seedlings and propagates the more unusual plants from cuttings.

The perfect balance of the park and garden, sheltered by the great ramparts of its ancient castle, is an elegant expression of the taste of its owners.

It has a very special atmosphere: here, as in few other places, I am made aware of the infinite scope of the garden as a creative medium, and of the extent to which a particular planting scheme can exert an influence over one's feelings, ideas, and sensibility.

BEDS OF S<small>ALVIA</small> <u>SPLENDENS</u> WITH THE RETAINING WALL COVERED IN GERANIUMS.

BOTTOM: COLEUS VARIETIES IN THE SUNKEN GARDEN.
TOP: THE LONG AVENUE OF CYPRESSES UNDERPLANTED WITH IMPATIENS.
LEFT: HOLM OAKS, OLIVES, CYPRESSES, AND MAGNOLIAS ALONG THE
PATH TO THE OLD RUINED FORTRESS.

MAROCCO DI VENEZIA

*The informal garden of Conte and
Contessa Giovanni Nuvoletti is set like a jewel
in the Venetian lagoon*

To arrive at the green entrance gate of Marocco di Venezia after driving through the Venetian hinterland along a busy provincial road lined with modern buildings is a strangely disorientating experience: behind the gate stretches a long, majestic avenue of linden trees hedged with cherry laurel and 'Mutabilis' roses and softened by convallaria, leading, at the far end, to the historic eighteenth-century house which was once the property of the Counts Papadopoli. Its windows shaded by blue blinds and decorated with cascades of pale pink geraniums, this small jewel is the perfect expression of the grace and charm of the Veneto. It was in this house, on 24 August 1849, that Venice's capitulation to the Habsburg Empire was signed, the act that

ABOVE: THE AVENUE OF WESTERN PLANES INTERSPERSED WITH STANDS OF RED ROSES.
RIGHT: THE MAIN AVENUE LEADING TO THE HOUSE WITH CHERRY LAUREL, AND LINDEN TREES.

THE AVENUE TO THE MAIN ROAD AS SEEN FROM THE FIRST FLOOR OF THE VILLA.

marked the end of the Republic of St Mark, and its surrender to the troops of Marshal Radetzky. A tablet set in the front wall of the house commemorates this sad event.

Conte Giovanni Nuvoletti and Contessa Clara Nuvoletti Agnelli bought this property on the Venetian mainland fifty years ago, when the area was still open countryside, consisting largely of fields of grain divided by long rows of poplars along their boundary ditches. The park covers about thirty hectares and was conceived and designed by its present owners, whose taste and imagination it reflects; just as a garden should be, it is a mirror of their own personalities, and its atmosphere is the result of a planting scheme devised specifically to create an impression of serenity and enchantment. Nothing has been designed, there are no precise patterns, just subtle hazes of color among the trees.

At the end of the central avenue of linden trees, planted when work on the garden began, a large, round rose bed containing two holm oaks (*Quercus ilex*) and four big pots spilling over with 'Sea Foam' roses like a waterfall, surround an elegant fountain in the shape of an obelisk. The entire property is crossed by long avenues of poplar trees that line the canals fed by the Terraglio river, running diagonally like green rays from the house to the countryside. An avenue of Western planes (*Platanus occidentalis*) follows the line of the railings on the east side of the house, which are completely covered by old garden roses and edged with lavender and an unusual mixed border, planted inside the boxes that are generally used for early sowings. Here delphiniums, aquilegia, and roses flower in abundance, and Contessa Nuvoletti explains that after they have been pruned the boxes are closed with sheets of glass, which protect the plants from winter frosts.

Behind the railings, the roses are mixed with magnificent hydrangeas. A central gate, framed by two large pots of white azaleas, leads to an inner garden dominated by an immense maple and a *Magnolia grandiflora*. The lawn below stretches as far as a large pergola, which is supported by tall iron arches and covered with *Wisteria sinensis* in three different colors – white, pink, and lilac – like a vaulted ceiling painted with an exquisite fresco from the studio of the Venetian Guardi brothers, who began the tradition of flower paintings in the eighteenth century. In the shade of the wisteria are large vases of *Osmanthus fragrans* and gardenias (*Gardenia jasminoides*) which fill the air with perfume, like a scented hothouse.

To the right of the pergola, the avenue of plane trees continues as far as the entrance gate to the great wood; with the route marked by large earthenware pots of

STANDARD ROSES.

ROSES IN THE OLD GARDEN.

romantic pale pink antique trailing roses which contrast effectively with the deep green of the trees.

The rose garden, bounded by a hedge of Pink Groot-endorst roses, their petals serrated like pinks or carnations, has a superb range of rose varieties and colors, though white is predominant. The Veneto region is famous for the cultivation of roses, both because of its loamy soil and because of the strong horticultural tradition in the north-east of Italy. A fountain surrounded by violas and lilies of the valley gives this corner of the garden a delightfully romantic air, which is accentuated by rows of fruit trees planted in an orderly pattern among the roses. Nearby, large patches of impatiens cover the ground in the shade of the trees.

From the rose garden a long avenue of poplars leads to the park where, for the pleasure of creating a new landscape, a small lake has been laid out; it is now carpeted with water lilies (*Nymphaea alba*) and pink lotuses (*Nelumbo nucifera*). The tall trees on the hill above lend height and movement to the flat Veneto landscape describing gentle curves on the horizon, and yet more rows of poplars can be seen in the background, marking the boundary of the estate. It is easy to see that in the park simplicity has been regarded as an end in itself: everything is linear and uncomplicated, with a skillful and imaginative use of space and color. Conte and Contessa

Nuvoletti were determined to create their garden without help from anyone else, expressing their own tastes, and above all respecting the landscape around them. It took a firm and steady hand to draw the straight, simple lines of the endless avenues of poplars, lindens, and planes which run across the property, and they are an extremely impressive feature of this serene and peaceful garden: it is a perfect place for walking and meditating; nothing clashes, and the plants thrive happily as a result of the attention and care that is lavished on them.

To the right of the avenue a vast lawn extends in front of the lake, enclosed at the end by a screen of trees, among them a number of splendid red maples whose flame red foliage in the fall enlivens the cool, encircling green. Here there are more large beds of roses, whose soft but intense colors seem to reflect not only the spirit of the Veneto landscape but also the joy and love that have gone into the making of this remarkable garden by a couple who have devoted their lives to its creation.

ABOVE: A BORDER OF WHITE ASTILBES,
FERNS AND WHITE CYCLAMEN FRAME A SMALL FOUNTAIN.
LEFT: POPLARS FRAME THE ''PARK'' CONTAINING SPECIMEN TREES WITH
THE OCCASIONAL ROSE BED GROWING AS IF NATURALLY.

VILLA EMO CAPODILISTA

On the Euganean hills a blend of
the classic and romantic created by Contessa
Marina Emo Capodilista

A dense screen of poplars lining the road that leads from Padua to Battaglia Terme conceals one of the most elegant and well-tended gardens in the Veneto region: the garden of Villa Emo Capodilista in the little hamlet of Rivella. The villa, itself a building of rare grace and elegance, is attributed to Vincenzo Scamozzi, an architect of the late sixteenth century and a pupil of Andrea Palladio.

Conte and Contessa Andrea Emo Capodilista, set out to create what they described as a "modern" Italian-style garden around the house: a garden in harmony with the classical spirit of the building and at the same time a place where they can give free rein to their own inspiration and imagination. The

ABOVE: THE MIDSUMMER SUN SETTING THROUGH THE VILLA.
RIGHT: ROSES, IRISES, HEMEROCALLIS, AND BERGENIAS FILL THE BORDER.

THE BOX PARTERRE.

prevailing sense of order and serenity gives way in parts of the garden to open spaces filled with pattern and color, the classical tradition of the Cinquecento contrasting with ideas inspired by the free forms of English Romanticism.

It was in 1966 that Conte and Contessa Emo Capodilista began work here, laying out a garden where before there had been nothing but vineyards and fields of maize. To complement the elegant classical lines of the main façade, they traced out their initials in an embroidery of box hedges, reviving what had once been a tradition of the Italian-style garden. Between the hedges, fine pink gravel from the Euganean hills nearby contrasts with the white river gravel along the edges of the paths. Alongside the "parterre", large beds of roses in colors shading from the white of 'Iceberg' to the pink of 'Queen Elizabeth' and 'Mona Lisa' border the two sixteenth-century fishponds, which were carefully restored in those early years; today they are two brilliant sheets of water, filled with carp that nestle in small niches set into the sides. This scene of great order and symmetry is enlivened in the months of May and June by the colors of the water arums, water hyacinths (*Eichhornia crassipes*), flag irises, and numerous water lilies that fill the ponds.

The back of the house looks onto a completely different scene. In contrast to the formal, circumscribed patterns of the parterres, rose beds, and fishponds, the garden here is an open, level expanse, like the Veneto landscape around it. Along the outer edge of the great central lawn runs a gallery of hornbeams, a feature typical of the gardens of the region. My friend Marina Emo Capodilista, daughter of Conte Andrea, took over the garden in 1978 and has enriched it with an enormous variety of new species, including a range of woodland plants that she has collected over the years. The cool promenade under the gallery of hornbeams has been given over to plants indigenous to the Euganean hills, with the result that even in winter, while the rest of the garden sleeps, flowers bloom beneath the hornbeams: snowdrop, *Scilla bifolia*, lungwort (*Pulmonaria officianalis*), green hellebore (*Helleborus viridis*), *Hepatica nobilis*, grape hyacinth (*Muscari neglectum*), meadow saffron, *Corydalis cava*, and wood anemone.

The hornbeams form a horseshoe-shaped boundary to this part of the garden, which is interrupted by a small semicircular pavilion covered by an enormous wisteria, providing a delicate touch of color amid the pale green leaves. A long pink and yellow border of mixed irises, roses, and hemerocallis, edged by a green "frill" of broad, wavy bergenia leaves, runs between the hornbeams and a second small pavilion, which is covered with white and pink roses.

ROSES CLIMBING AGAINST A FRESH WHITE WALL.

LARGE BEDS OF ROSES AND CLIMBING ROSES
LEAD TOWARDS THE EUGANIAN HILLS.

I have always thought that one of the garden's most spectacular features is a royal crown of flowers, an immense bed of the celebrated rose 'Paul Neyron', created in Lyon by Antoine Levet in 1869, which produces enormous double pink flowers with lilac highlights; the color is so distinctive that it is now known as "Neyron rose".

In the center of the lawn is a basin filled not with aquatic plants, but with winter-flowering bergenias. The imagination and creativity of Contessa Marina are clearly evident in the extremely long mixed borders that run down two sides of the lawn, at right angles to the villa. Here a series of perennials have been planted to ensure continuous flowering from March to October. The skill that has gone into selecting the plants for this border is reflected in the changing shades that appear at different seasons of the year. At Villa Emo Capodilista each month has its own colors, like bursts of fireworks: white, blue, pink, yellow, and brown irises mix with soft patches of

BOTTOM: LONG MIXED BORDERS RUNNING ALONGSIDE THE LAWN.
TOP: 'PAUL NEYRON' ROSES AND THE FAMILY DOG.
LEFT: THE REAR OF THE HOUSE.

primroses, narcissi, and candytuft; lupins, lavender, and columbines with love-in-a-mist (nigella); calamint, peonies, and valerian with astilbe, yarrows, horehounds, phlomis, and orpines (sedum); splendid deep blue tufts of *Anchusa azurea* with sky blue delphiniums and perovskia. The plants are allowed to multiply and mix in an easy disorder that contrasts with the cool expanse of the lawn and the hornbeam gallery, introducing movement and gaiety into the dull monotony of the Veneto landscape.

Another, more secluded, walk still remains to be discovered: a long avenue of magnolias that leads from the house to a watercourse, which widens out to form a miniature lake. Large orange patches of hemerocallis and flowering pomegranate provide a counterpoint to the measured rhythm of the magnolias while, on the left, a long canal, bordered entirely by creamy white *Iris orientalis*, runs alongside the avenue as far as the little lake, set in the shade of weeping willows and dense groves of bamboo. The subtle matching of bamboo and willow leaves in identical shades of green, combined with the vivid yellows and oranges, is one of the most beautiful sights in the garden. The interplay of colors brings an element of magic to the serried rows of poplars, the long fishponds, and the flat terrain, enhancing rather than disturbing the classical balance of the scheme.

Contessa Marina Emo Capodilista is now the owner of the villa and devotes much of her time to tending her garden, working unceasingly with a deep and genuine passion in order to bring back to life one of the most colorful and flower-filled gardens in the Veneto.

There is a sentence in Sir George Sitwell's famous book *An Essay on the Making of Gardens* that perfectly describes the view through the great wrought-iron gate at *Villa Emo Capodilista*:

"So, to man the garden should be something without and beyond nature; a page from an old romance, a scene in fairyland, a gateway through which imagination lifting above the sombre realities of life may pass into a world of dreams."

WHITE IRIS ORIENTALIS RUN ALONGSIDE A LONG CANAL.

VILLA DEI PIOPPI

The ancient botanical garden of
Benedetto and Maria Luisa Sgaravatti in the
"Garden City" of Padua

The city of Padua has played a vital role in the history of gardening. It is the home of the oldest botanical garden in the world, created in 1545; originally known as the Orto dei Semplici, it has been perfectly preserved, retaining the original structure characteristic of that time. Goethe admired it when he visited Padua in 1786, and has left us an account of his impressions in his *Italian Journey*.

Benedetto and Maria Luisa Sgaravatti's garden lies in the part of Padua now known as the "Garden City", where remains of the old city walls once stood, together with a tower dating from 1300 which formed an important part of the city's defenses. Beneath the tower a large gate called the "Porta del

ABOVE: WINDOW BOXES AND BORDERS LEAD TO THE MEDIEVAL TOWER.
LEFT: VIEW THROUGH THE TWO GREAT ARCHES.

Soccorso" (Gate of Reinforcements) was used to bring in troops when the city was under attack.

In 1807 a huge garden was created here by a great plant lover, Antonio Piazza, who laid out a majestic avenue of plane trees alternating with statues, leading to an exotic arboretum. The fourteenth-century tower, which is still standing, gave the place that medieval flavor which was so eagerly striven for in other gardens of the period. Inside the tower was a museum of memorial tablets, bas-reliefs, coats of arms, and columns, and in the courtyard stood a statue of the Callipygean Venus, goddess of beauty, on a marble column. A passage covered by a trellis of vines led from the second floor of the tower, along the top of the old walls to a small temple dedicated to Apollo. Naturally, an essential feature of the garden was a maze, which was set at the bottom of a flight of steps so that the labyrinth of hedges could be viewed from above. Avenues of hornbeams, statues, and hedges of roses helped to create a happy blend of traditional elements of both the Italian-style and the English-style garden, which was then coming into vogue.

Unfortunately, all that remains of Piazza's creation are a number of contemporary prints, a handwritten guide which he compiled himself, and a few ancient plants. In 1900, the park was turned into a riding school and was used as such until Benedetto Sgaravatti transformed it into the garden to be seen there today.

Sgaravatti bears a historic name in the botanical world: his ancestors have been gardeners since the eighteenth century and in 1900, the family established itself as the largest and most widespread firm of nurserymen in Italy. A landscapist, garden designer, and president of the Commission for the Preservation of the Veneto Landscape, his knowledge, experience, and passion for the world of plants have contributed to the creation of many parkland areas in Italy.

Benedetto Sgaravatti acquired the property in 1938, and the house dates from that period; built in the typical Fascist style, imposing and simple at one and the same time, it is framed by a garden that effectively sets off its

THE COURTYARD OF THE TOWER WITH ITS ANCIENT DRINKING FOUNTAIN.

RIGHT: CORDYLINE ENVELOPED BY PANSIES AND GERANIUMS.
TOP AND BOTTOM LEFT: IMPATIENS AND LOBELIAS IN AN ANCIENT STONE VASE.

architecture. On one side, the property is bounded by a row of white poplars (*Populus alba*) (*pioppi* means poplar in Italian – hence the name of the villa), which form a natural wall, isolating it from the rest of the city, while along the other side it borders the Bacchiglione, the river that runs through Padua. One is immediately aware on entering the garden that the splendors of the nineteenth-century park have left a permanent imprint here, as if the memories of the past live on in the new garden.

Inside the entrance gate, a three-meter high hedge of yew (*Taxus baccata*) alternating with umbrella pine (*Pinus pinea*) and *Cupressus arizonica* separates the main garden from the orchard, where perfectly straight rows of apples, pears, apricots, peaches, and cherries enclose a small central fountain.

On the right-side, in front of the house, a broad expanse of lawn is bordered by a hedge of pink and blue *Hydrangea macrophylla*. *Viburnum odoratissimum*, *Spiraea* x *vanhouttei*, *Cornus alba*, and an elegant clump of *Hibiscus moscheutos* form a group of plants well suited to the local climate, which is very damp during the winter.

The lawn stretches as far as the medieval tower, interrupted only by a path that runs round the house. A variety of trees and shrubs such as hornbeam (*Carpinus betulus*), copper beech (*Fagus sylvatica* 'Atropurpurea'), Lombardy poplar (*Populus nigra* 'Italica'), variegated weigela, and the hybrid black poplar (*Populus* x *canadensis*) form a dense screen enclosing the lawn. The tower itself is framed by splendid ancient poplars, holm oaks, and an enormous box-elder (*Acer negundo*), and its walls are covered with Virginia creeper (*Parthenocissus quinquefolia*), which turns a brilliant flame red in the fall. Along the two great arches that support the ancient fortifications is an impressive collection of azaleas, their red, pink, white, and violet flowers standing out dramatically against the old stones; the spring-flowering azaleas are interspersed with *Hydrangea macrophylla*. Up a few steps is the courtyard of the tower where magnificent red roses, along with geraniums and impatiens, flower almost continuously underneath the arches. An ancient drinking

AN IMPRESSIVE F̲I̲C̲U̲S̲ E̲L̲A̲S̲T̲I̲C̲A̲.

fountain in the middle, frequently visited by pigeons, relieves the severity of the courtyard. From a stone bench nearby one can sit and admire the delightfully romantic view of medieval ruins, centuries-old trees, and the river lined with willows, whose branches trail in the water below the tower. There is even a small landing-stage for rowing on the river.

I think the most distinctive feature of the garden is its continuous display of color throughout the year. In spring, the beds around the house and on the patio are planted with pansies (*Viola tricolor*), primroses, and forget-me-nots (*Myosotis* spp.), and over the summer months marigolds, impatiens, ageratums, petunias, and geraniums come into flower in turn, spreading along the flight of steps that leads down from the patio. Enclosing the patio itself are white columns festooned with 'Fashion', 'New Dawn', 'Comtesse Vandal', 'Queen Elizabeth', and 'Crimson Glory' roses, making a magnificent display of color against the immense green expanse of the lawn. Even the large windows of the house are framed by pots of petunias and small begonias, while *Clematis* 'Pamela Jackman' and *Clematis montana rubens* cover the side of the house least exposed to the sun.

Until a few years ago, I remember a huge oriental plant (*Platanus orientalis*) standing in front of the tower,

dominating the whole garden. Now all that is left as a reminder of its enormous size is its stump, which is covered with brightly colored geraniums and petunias.

To the south of the tower, the ground slopes up to form a hill crowned by a large holm oak, whose spreading branches make an area of cool shade. Small violets grow along the steps that climb the hillside, and from the top there is a superb view over the whole garden: though simple in design, it has a majesty that derives both from its magnificent trees and from the ruins of the ancient walls that surround the tower, and from this vantage point the vista is unparalleled in the whole of Padua.

ABOVE: ACER PALMATUM 'DISSECTUM ATROPURPUREUM'.
RIGHT: THE PATIO WITH LOGGIA AND ORNAMENTAL POOL.

VILLA LOREDAN

Flowering plants and trees magnificently blended with the Venetian landscape by Bruno and Anita Saccomani

Any lover of gardens finding himself in Noventa Padovana, a few kilometers from the city of Padua, would be pleasantly surprised to discover a villa there that dates from the sixteenth century, a time when this part of the Veneto – now one of the most industrialized regions in Europe – was almost entirely covered by ancient forests. Such were the riches of the Veneto forests that the German emperor Frederick Barbarossa spent much of his time hunting in the woods along the river Brenta between battles in his Italian campaign. Another great hunting enthusiast was Crown Prince Umberto, later Umberto I of Savoia, who was a guest at Villa Loredan in 1870.

The villa has belonged for centuries to an old family of the Veneto

ABOVE: A VIEW OF THE VILLA FROM THE CORNER OF THE LAWN.
LEFT: A MIXED BORDER ALONGSIDE THE LAWN FEATURING HEMEROCALLIS AND DELPHINIUMS.

A PAIR OF SPECIMEN LIQUIDAMBAR STYRACIFLUA.

bourgeoisie, always handed down from uncle to nephew as there were never any direct descendants (Bruno and Anita Saccomani are the first for many generations to have children). During the eighteenth century, in particular, the family built a number of summer retreats, small hunting lodges, and villas in the area, which are described so effectively by Goldoni in his comedy in three acts *Le smanie per la villeggiatura* (The Mania for Vacations), which was performed for the first time in 1761 and was followed by *Le avventure della villeggiatura* (Adventures on

Vacation) and *Ritorno dalla villeggiatura* (Return from Vacation).

As early as the fifteenth century Leon Battista Alberti had written:

"I would like the houses in the possession of nobles not to be set in the most fertile parts of the countryside, but in the most appropriate, where every amenity can be found; that they may look out over the towns, the lands, the sea, and an expanse of plain, and the familiar peaks of the hills and the mountains."

The simple Villa Loredan was enlarged and transformed in the eighteenth century, and decorated inside with fine Venetian-style stuccos, dating from 1775. The great park was created in the same year, with its dense wood of hornbeams, a tree much in vogue in the Venetian gardens of the time. The wood fulfilled a precise function in the overall concept of the Italian garden, not only providing shelter from the sun but also offering an effective contrast to the geometric patterns of the parterre; in that eighteenth-century world, due respect was paid to "virgin, untouched" nature, and a mass of greenery provided the ideal natural backdrop for the villa, which was often built close to the edge of the wood, at the point where the open landscape began.

The garden of Villa Loredan covers an area of three hectares and is made up of two distinct sections: one planted in 1945 in the midst of what remains of the old hornbeam wood and the other created recently by Signora Saccomani to a design by Henry Cocker. Large hornbeams, beeches, planes, and poplars form a semicircle in front of the villa, carpeting the great lawn with golden leaves in the fall, and a small balustraded external staircase decorated with vases of African lilies (*Agapanthus africanus*) ornaments the main façade: the effect is gentle and soft, like everything in the Veneto, where the character of the landscape is reflected in the style of the houses and gardens. A tall poplar hedge, planted on the former site of a vineyard, separates the old garden from the new; the new one consists of a large lawn bounded at the rear by an interesting variety of trees, including sweet

A MIXED BORDER OF <u>STACHYS</u> <u>LANATA</u>, DELPHINIUMS AND HEMEROCALLIS.

gum, holm oak, *Acer saccharum*, weeping beech, *Betula pendula*, and a great variety of maples, which grow to their full height and size in the humid climate and acid soil of the region. Along the left-hand side of the lawn runs a long mixed border made up of bearded iris, one of this garden's specialities, narcissi, day lilies of various colors, *Phlox paniculata*, and *Kniphofia pumila*, interspersed with a fine collection of bush roses, making a broad band of color in a delightfully delicate blend of different shades: Signora Saccomani's garden must surely have one of the best displays of flowers in Padua.

In front of the lawn, interrupted by a broad gravel path running right round the villa, I particularly love a superb collection of hydrangeas – *H. macrophylla* 'Lanarth White', *H. paniculata* 'Grandiflora', *H. macrophylla* 'Mariesii' (syn. *H.* 'Blue Wave'), and *H.* 'Ayesha' – grouped against a screen of trees and shrubs, which makes a particularly effective backdrop during the hot

summer months, when the hydrangeas are in flower.

At the back of the villa is another, smaller garden, laid out around a central path lined with irises and roses and encircled by magnolias, *Osmanthus fragrans*, a large cedar of Lebanon, and several pines. This romantic corner of the garden, where the plants have been carefully chosen so that they bloom in continuous succession, is filled with flowers and scent throughout most of the year.

Although Villa Loredan is not counted among the great villas of the Brenta, as are its close neighbors the Malcontenta and Villa Pisani, the importance of its garden increases with every passing year. In an area that has now been almost completely taken over by industry, it is an invaluable survivor of a vanished civilization, a

civilization of which the villas of the Veneto are almost the only remaining relics. The present generation of Paduans, surrounded by mechanization and technology, can only look back with nostalgia to a time when man was able to commune directly with nature.

Bruno Saccomani is a lawyer and one of the best known personalities in Padua, not only in legal circles but also in those of culture and politics; he has an abiding love of nature, and especially of trees, and this, combined with his wife's passion for flowers, has been his main motivation both in keeping intact this corner of the Veneto and in enhancing its gentle serenity through the introduction of new species and the addition of a magnificent collection of flowering plants.

BOTTOM: STACHYS BYZANTINA (S. LANATA) IN ONE OF THE BORDERS.
TOP: A MASS OF PINK HYDRANGEAS CONTRASTING WITH THE DEEP RED GERANIUMS.
LEFT: HYDRANGEA ARBORESCENS 'GRANDIFLORA' AND ACER PALMATUM 'DISSECTUM PURPUREUM'.

VILLA RIZZARDI

*In an eighteenth-century garden
Contessa Cristina Guerrieri Rizzardi preserves
a green amphitheater*

A few kilometers from Verona, in the heart of the Valpolicella, an area renowned for its wines and for the charm of its landscape, stands the Villa Rizzardi, whose Italian-style garden was laid out at the end of the eighteenth century. One of the last of its kind to be created, it already shows signs of the English influence that was growing ever stronger at that time as a result of trade links between Italy and Great Britain. British and Italian gardening styles were in sharp contrast, yet the English who made their homes in Italy – most of them in Tuscany – succeeded in fusing the two ideals, stripping away the geometric lines of the formal Italian garden in favour of wide stretches of lawn and decorative trees. In the garden of Villa Rizzardi the symmetrical

ABOVE: A TEA HOUSE DETAIL. RIGHT: THE HORNBEAM AVENUE.

flower beds, the terraces, the central axis linking the house to the theater, and the belvedere looking out over the landscape are typically Italian; Anglo-Saxon elements include the wide expanses of lawn, the wood, and above all a whole new range of plants imported from China, Japan, and India, as was the fashion in England at the end of the eighteenth century. The garden owes its blend of styles to the simple fact that the owner of the villa, Conte Antonio Rizzardi, was a merchant of Verona who had spent many years of his life in far-off countries and had married an Englishwoman.

The villa was rebuilt in the second half of the nineteenth century and is at present occupied by the Spanish sculptor Miguel Berrocal. The garden, on the other hand, dates from 1783, and was designed by Luigi Trezza, whose original drawings can be seen today in the Biblioteca Civica in Verona.

It was laid out behind the villa, along the side of a hill, and was constructed, in accordance with baroque principles, on three levels – linked together by long avenues of cypresses – in order to take full advantage of the view. At the side of the villa is a small *giardino segreto*, carved out of the hillside, with a delightful variety of rare and scented plants, and a little waterfall. It is connected to the second floor of the building by a bridge, which provides direct access to it from the main bedroom.

A visit to the garden begins at the caretaker's house at the top; a small path runs down from there to a flight of stone steps, which leads in turn to a classic Italian-style parterre with geometric box hedges surrounding a circular basin. To the right, on the second level, tall evergreen espaliers enclose the circular "lemon garden", decorated with lemon trees in terracotta vases; a lemon house, once used to shelter the plants in winter, has now been transformed into a pleasant tea house.

Beyond the parterre, in a direct line with the villa, runs a wide tunnel of hornbeams, a feature typical of Veneto gardens, though here the trees have been pruned to leave an open space above, so that the narrow shafts of light pour down to brighten the path between them. The

A VIEW OVER THE PARTERRE.

A SECTION OF THE PARTERRE SHOWING SHAPED HEDGES, STATUES AND CYPRESSES.

tunnel culminates in a niche containing a statue, surrounded by four large cypresses. An avenue of immense, majestic cypresses, rather curiously interspersed with *Yucca constricta*, leads on from this point to the green theater, the largest of its kind in Italy, whose entrance is guarded by two stone lions. It is an amphitheater carved out of the hillside and enclosed by a tall hedge, a series of statues stand in niches chipped out of the hedge and the seats are trimmed hedges of box. It was created in 1796, when work on the rest of the garden was complete.

To the left of the theater, the cypress avenue resumes its progress, running up a gentle slope to frame one of the most impressive features of the garden, the belvedere. This octagonal gray stone building, surrounded by a balustrade decorated with *putti*, has a central staircase that divides in two, with a statue at the center. The stone of the belvedere glows like a jewel against the green of the trees that enclose it. The whole valley of Negrar, from the vineyards below the garden to the far horizon, opens up from this spectacular viewpoint.

Beyond the belvedere stretches the wood, the most secluded and romantic part of the whole garden. Originally it was made up of oaks, but sadly they were felled after the signing of the treaty of Campoformio in 1797, when the territories of Verona and the Valpolicella were annexed by the Austrian empire. Other species have now grown up in their place, elms for the most part, which surround a circular chamber open to the sky; used

GEOMETRIC BOX HEDGES, STATUE AND A STONE POOL.

occasionally as a dining room in the hottest days of summer, this stone building was conceived as a ruin, the internal walls covered with tufa and decorated with statues; I remember some wonderful meals here, a tracery of elm branches forming a green dome which looks almost like a painted ceiling. The trees extend all around it, sheltering a strange assortment of stone animals in the undergrowth, which add a degree of mystery to the enigmatic silence of the wood. One of the plants that make up this undergrowth is the small palm *Trachycarpus fortunei*, a plant that will grow almost anywhere.

The historic original garden of Villa Rizzardi has largely been kept intact. The present owner, Contessa Cristina, has even succeeded in preserving the magical atmosphere of the open-air performances that were one of the delights of the Veneto nobility at the end of the eighteenth century, and it is not hard today to imagine the sound of flutes wafting from the belvedere.

No doubt the Contessa would endorse the words of Charles-Joseph de Ligne, owner of the famous contemporary garden of Beloeil, which was known, admired, and envied by half the courts of Europe:

"I could consider myself happy if, by beautifying nature or drawing closer to it, or, better still, by making its presence felt, I were able to make people love it; from our gardens this would lead us elsewhere; . . . and the Gods, a hundred times happier than on Olympus, would beg men to let them join them."

117

BOTTOM: STRANGE STONE ANIMALS IN THE UNDERGROWTH.
TOP: THE CIRCULAR STONE CHAMBER WITH ITS STATUES.
LEFT: ONE OF THE TWO STONE LIONS GUARDING THE ENTRANCE TO THE GREEN THEATER.

VILLA VOTALARCA

*Water spurts in the enchanted park of Marchese
and Marchesa Gianfranco and Elena Luzi*

The landscape of Macerata, with its gently undulating hills, its patchwork of woods and fields of grain, is probably more typical of the Marches than that of any other province in the region. Goethe had words of praise for the Marches too: "But you must not picture it as a desert. Though mountainous, it is well cultivated, the chestnuts thrive, the wheat is excellent, and the crops are green already. The road is bordered with evergreen oaks, and around the churches and chapels stand slender cypresses . . .".

Villa Votalarca stands on a hill in the district of Treja, not far from the city of Macerata. The road to it runs parallel to the Potenza river, and at a certain point a large group of buildings, with the villa at its center, comes into view.

ABOVE: A BUST OF A WOMAN STANDS GUARD OVER THE ENTRANCE TO THE BAROQUE BASIN.
LEFT: THE BAROQUE BASIN WITH ITS SMALL TEMPLE CONTAINING A STATUE OF NEPTUNE.

It is enclosed by a large park, covering about six hectares. The villa faces onto a lawn like a vast green piazza, with an obelisk bordered by flower beds at the center; it is surrounded by a wall of trees – cedars, firs, elms, olives, and planes – many of which are hundreds of years old. To the right is an Italian-style garden, sheltered by tall pines and set at a lower level than the great lawn. A gravel path runs down this long, narrow strip flanked by box hedges about half a meter high, which enclose flowering shrubs such as *Forsythia* × *intermedia*, *Spiraea* × *vanhouttei*, *Berberis* × *ottawensis* 'Superba', and old garden roses. The path is intersected by a tunnel of *Rosa banksiae lutea*, which leads to a rotunda on the left, surrounded by bamboo.

In front of the main façade of the villa are two winter gardens enclosed by tall hedges and filled with old garden roses; here a small greenhouse and a lemon house are used to shelter delicate plants from the harsh winter weather.

The most curious and distinctive feature of the garden, however, is the wood, where ornamental fountains and *giochi d'acqua* are concealed among the trees, almost as if the god Pan were lying in wait to catch unwary visitors with jets of water, which spurt suddenly from unexpected places. "These great Italians have learned to play with water the way a sultan plays with his jewels, the way Turner played with light", wrote Sir George Sitwell in his book *On the Making of Gardens*. It is a talent that dates back to the seventeenth century, when advances in hydraulics allowed immensely sohisticated and complex mechanisms to be introduced on a vast scale in baroque gardens of the period.

A gate with pillars surmounted by two eagles marks the entrance to the wood where the great, sunlit space of the lawn immediately gives way to the dense shade of ancient elms, laurels, holm oaks, cork oaks, pines, lindens, and bamboo. The trees are thinned out every three years while the undergrowth is pruned every year.

The wood covers an area of five thousand square meters and was laid out by Marchese Nicola Luzi, who began work on it in 1830 and completed it in 1851.

Near the entrance, a baroque basin bordered by gray

RAMBLER ROSES SURROUNDING THE BASE OF A PALM TREE.

A broad, winding drive lined with trees cuts a swathe through a dense wood of holm oaks and pines to emerge in front of the house, where it crosses a straight central avenue that runs downhill from the main façade: this avenue is flanked by stone lions and boxwood hedges and bordered by more holm oaks, palm trees, and bamboo.

The villa, which is surrounded by farm buildings, farmworkers' cottages, a steward's house and a church – the church of the Madonna della Misericordia – was built in 1737 to the design of Angelo Maria Nucelli. It was restored in 1927 and has retained its original character as a fortified country residence in spite of having acquired a neoclassical pediment.

ONE OF THE PATHWAYS RUNNING THROUGH THE WOOD.

stone and *Ruscus hypoglossum* reflects the image of a small temple, with a statue of Neptune close by, seated on the head of a sea monster from whose mouth spurts a long jet of water. A narrow gravel path leads to a second fountain, where ancient Roman relics are set into a "Greco-Roman" temple. In the nineteenth century, all large gardens were adorned with fragments of ancient buildings and sculptures; they were easy to obtain, and Marchese Nicola Luzi made full use of them in this, the most whimsical of gardens.

The walk continues between columns and amphorae, which are effectively set off by the surrounding greenery. In the middle of the wood stands a knoll crowned with a small Chinese pagoda; it is reached by way of a path over a bridge, which leads from the Roman relics to the viewpoint on the summit. A grotto known as the "Sibilla Eritrea" has been carved out of the knoll, with its entrance guarded by two owls. Inside is a sculpture of the Sybil by Venanzio Bigioli (1839). At the foot of the grotto is an enormous holm oak which forms an integral part of it, as if nature itself had been infected by the prevailing spirit of fantasy.

The light filters through the dense foliage of the trees and lends an air of magic and enchantment to the pathway. So powerful is its spell that one might easily believe that the wooden figure of a gardener, peering out of the

THE RUINS OF THE TEMPLE OF APOLLO.

doorway of her little house with a bunch of flowers in her hands is real; outside, a stone statue of a girl, clothed in moss, looks on. Could the roundabout, which has survived intact, with its sea horses and sirens, have been placed there to amuse these motionless figures?

Suddenly the mood changes: set out along the "path of the tombs" are monuments with stone tablets and inscriptions, Roman busts, funeral effigies, urns, and the tomb of Marchesa Maria Anna, wife of the man from whose imagination all this sprang. Again, without warning, tiny but well-aimed jets of water spurt out and catch the visitor unprepared, or a hunter, concealed among the trees, shoots unexpectedly at the wild boar in front of him . . . with water, naturally. Another essential feature of such a fanciful world is of course an aviary for turtle doves. An obelisk in the "Egyptian square" points the way to the little church of the Hermit, where a venerable old man carved out of wood fasts and prays. A path winds its way into the dense wood, to a group of statues depicting innocent virgins looking pointedly away from the bacchanals and oriental dancing women nearby. Further on are the ruins of the temple of Apollo and the sixteenth-century castle in which a melancholy prisoner is confined: I remember once approaching the iron bars in a spirit of sympathy for this suffering figure, and treacherous jets of water shot from below, soaking me to the skin.

This great nineteenth-century flight of fancy terminates in a long tunnel, completely covered with ivy, which leads back to the main garden. The water for the *giochi d'acqua* is drawn from the Potenza river and stored in wells inside the little buildings dotted throughout the wood; the pipes, which date back to 1911, are still in perfect condition. Returning to the bright expanse of the lawn, one cannot fail to wonder at the brilliance of the garden's designer, a man of childlike playfulness and inspired imagination who created a strange, spirited fantasy world that has survived intact for over a century. It is an extremely rare example of its kind, and its excellent state of preservation is the result of constant care and continuous maintenance work on the part of Gianfranco Luzi and his wife.

A MOSS-COVERED STONE STATUE OF A GIRL, THE GARDENER'S ASSISTANT, ASLEEP.

ABOVE RIGHT: THE LITTLE CHURCH OF THE HERMIT.
TOP LEFT: A CHILDREN'S MERRY-GO-ROUND.
BOTTOM LEFT: THE MELANCHOLY PRISONER OF THE CASTLE.

VILLA PONTIFICIA

The spectacular formal gardens of the papal summer retreat at Castel Gandolfo

In the superb setting of the Albani hills, about twenty-five kilometers from Rome, in one of the lushest parts of Lazio, rich with vineyards and surrounded by the Roman castles of Ariccia, Frascati, Marino, Genzano, and Velletri, is the small town of Castel Gandolfo, where the Pope has his summer residence, the Villa Pontificia. It became the summer retreat of the popes during the pontificate of Urban VIII (Cardinal Matteo Barberini, 1623–44), after whom it took its name of Villa Barberini. It was chosen both for its pleasant site overlooking Lake Albano and for the healthy climate of the hills in which it stands; at Castel Gandolfo it was possible to escape the malarial miasmas that, especially in the hottest months of summer, infested

ABOVE: THE PRIVATE GARDEN WITH THE STATUE OF THE ''MADONNINA'' IN HER SMALL TEMPLE.
RIGHT: THE LOWER AVENUE LEADING TO THE VILLA GUARDED BY SENTINEL CYPRESSES.

A PART OF THE ORIGINAL ROMAN VILLA WITH ITS ROMAN ROAD RUNNING ALONGSIDE.

Rome and its surrounding countryside. The Popes' example was followed by the most important Roman families, who set up sumptuous residences in the so-called "castelli", the group of ancient fortified towns to the south-east of the city. In this way the Pallavicino, Aldobrandini, Borghese, and many other aristocratic families of the time followed in the footsteps of the patricians of ancient Rome. (Cicero had a villa at Tusculum, near present-day Frascati, in the first century B.C.) Villa Barberini was used as a summer residence by various popes, including Alexander VII and Clement XI, and underwent extensive alterations between 1930 and 1932 at the behest of Pius XI. This took place after the signing of the Lateran Treaties in 1929, on the basis of which the lands belonging to the papal villa had been extended by the addition of an adjoining estate covering forty hectares, which incorporated part of the ancient Roman villa of the emperor Domitian, the last of the house of Flavius. This property had come into the possession of Urban VIII's nephew, the young Cardinal Taddeo Barberini, who had wanted to have a villa of his own at Castel Gandolfo, close to the papal residence, and had acquired the so-called Mompecchio estate in 1629.

The imperial villa of Domitian was laid out on a number of different levels and included a theater, the four nymphaea that are still visible today, and, on the side facing the sea, a long terrace over a cryptoporticus (vaulted promenade below ground level), which was surmounted by a colonnaded loggia.

In restructuring the summit residence, Pius XI wanted the new, modern building to respect the layout of the old villa, on which Bernini had worked between 1624 and 1629 for Urban VIII and later for Pope Alexander VII Chigi, though all that now remains of the seventeenth-century structure is the façade and a gateway in the wall of the garden, bearing the mountains and star of the Chigi coat of arms.

Today, the system of roads connecting the various parts of the property has been greatly extended and now covers about fourteen kilometers, while the grounds have been carefully laid out to provide panoramic views of the enchanting surrounding landscape.

As part of the rebuilding and restoration work, the villa was given a large stylized park on the upper terrace, and an extensive Italian-style garden on the lower one. At a slightly lower level still, an English-style garden – the "Giardino degli Specchi" (the Garden of Mirrors) – was laid out with green lawns around two lakes covered with water lilies and framed by box trimmed into the shapes of

THE VIEW DOWN FROM THE VILLA AND ALONG THE AVENUE OF CYPRESSES, ROSES, AND LAUREL HEDGES.

RIGHT: AN OLD STATUE LOCATED IN THE CENTRE OF THE EXEDRA.

THE PIAZZA QUADRATA.

globes and truncated pyramids. It is enclosed by a tall screen of cypresses that faces the fountain of Neptune, with pines, holm oaks, and more splendid cypresses as a backdrop. These three terraces, known together as the "Giardini del Belvedere", constitute the most important feature of the new park.

The first Italian-style garden is called the "Giardino della Magnolia" after the great pyramidal *Magnolia grandiflora* that stands at the center of a large Florentine fleur-de-lis, outlined in box and filled with seasonal flowers. The entrance to this garden is clearly marked by a fountain set at the top of a circular flight of steps and shaded by an ancient holm oak.

The focal point of the garden is the "parco" on the first terrace, which consists of sixteen large squares of grass bounded by box hedges. Inside the squares are magnificent old trees such as Atlas cedars, deodars (*Cedrus deodara*), majestic umbrella pines (*Pinus pinea*), an Irish yew and strawberry trees (*Arbutus unedo*), which have grown to a remarkable size in the microclimate of Castel Gandolfo. The mild winters have also allowed three splendid monkey puzzle trees (*Araucaria araucana*) to

THE "PARCO" IN THE FIRST TERRACE.

thrive here. The squares have been planted with camellias, gardenias, azaleas, and Chinese hibiscus, whose vivid colors stand out dramatically against the trees. In the summer, hydrangeas flower along an ancient Roman wall that bounds one side of the park. At the end of the park, holm oaks, laurels, and six majestic cypresses provide the setting for a statue of the "Madonnina" (little Madonna) in a small temple whose image is reflected in a pool ringed with water lilies.

Another terrace commands a fine view over the so-called "Piazza quadrata", a square enclosed by a screen of cypresses cut into the shape of a Roman aqueduct, ten cone-shaped holm oaks directing one's gaze out over the spectacular landscape to the Tyrrhenian Sea in the distance. The viewpoint on the terrace is linked to the "Piazza quadrata" by means of a staircase built around a fountain; a wall of *Trachelospermum jasminoides* decorates the top flight of steps, and the balustrades are lined with terracotta vases of *Pittosporum tobira*.

The most spectacular view of all, however, is from the belvedere overlooking the great Italian-style garden that extends for about three hundred meters along the second

terrace. The layout of the box hedges and flowering plants in this lavish parterre is reminiscent of the coffered ceiling of a Roman basilica. Tall cypresses surround this classically formal area, which culminates in an exedra housing an ancient statue. Along its entire length the garden is bordered on one side by the monumental Roman structure of Domitian's cryptoporticus, whose ancient wall is covered with the multicolored blooms of magnificent ramblers that climb right up to the balustrade. The words of Sir George Sitwell spring to mind: ". . . beauty arouses feeling, feeling opens the doors of the imagination, which is thus left free to wander through a world of dreams." The Italian-style garden runs without a break into a citrus orchard, where trees in splendid terracotta vases are set out on stone pedestals as soon as the winter is over.

The rest of the large estate is filled with lush orchards, ancient olive trees, and vast meadows that provide grazing for the cows of a model dairy; spacious terraces, carved by Herculean effort out of the stony ground, are used for the cultivation of vegetables. The abundant supply of water in the area, together with the warm climate and fertile soil (Lake Albano was once a volcanic crater), have encouraged plants of all kinds to grow at a remarkable rate and to achieve unusual size, a fact that has been

ABOVE: DETAIL OF STEPS LEADING BETWEEN THE PARTERRE GARDENS.
RIGHT: FROM THE BELVEDERE, TWO 1930S' SCULPTURES OVERSEE
THE VIEW ALONG THE GREAT ITALIAN GARDEN.

skilfully exploited by the papal gardeners over the course of three centuries.

Anyone who has the honor to be granted admission to the papal villa of Castel Gandolfo comes away enraptured, feeling rather as Dante Alighieri must have done when he reached the highest realms of heaven in his *Paradiso*. In fact, the villa is unique in bearing the mark of Roman emperors, cardinals and popes as well as having drawn on the talents of the greatest artists of the time in transforming its surroundings into a place of pure enchantment.

Its gardens, terraces, and park are laid out among magnificent Roman imperial remains, filled with sculptures thousands of years old, and ornamented with buildings designed by the best architects in Rome from the seventeenth century to the twentieth: there is no doubt that its great treasures, which were the inspiration for the engravings of Giovan Battista Piranesi, belong not to Italy alone but to the whole of humanity. Their creation and preservation have been the responsibility of all the popes of Rome who have had the good fortune to enjoy them, whether as a means of spiritual elevation for man or as a terrestrial image of paradise.

ABOVE: THE ORIGINAL ROMAN OUTER WALL.
LEFT: AN AVENUE OF UMBRELLA PINES AND CYPRESSES IN THE
LOWER PART OF THE PARK.

SAN LIBERATO

In the tranquil woodlands above Lake Bracciano
Contessa Maria Odescalchi Sanminiatelli
indulges her passion for roses

Sometimes it is possible to fall hopelessly in love with a place, especially if you have the soul of a gardener and an overriding love for plants. This is what happened to Conte Donato and Contessa Maria Odescalchi Sanminiatelli, who decided to create their garden on a large plot of land surrounded by chestnut woods above Lake Bracciano, an ancient volcanic crater near Rome. On the estate stood a small Romanesque church, San Liberato, which was the only building in that romantic and tranquil setting, with a hillside sloping gently down to the lake and the huge natural amphitheater of the woods enclosing it at the back. It was an ideal place to create a garden and to plant all the trees of which Conte Sanminiatelli had always dreamed.

ABOVE: THE SOUTH-EAST WALL OF THE HOUSE
COVERED WITH TRACHELOSPERMUM JASMINOIDES.
LEFT: ROSES, VALERIAN AND OLIVE TREES.

In 1964, the English landscape designer Russell Page was commissioned to lay out the garden, which extends from the woods to the lake, retaining large open spaces so that views were left clear and the natural character of the garden maintained. In one of his essays, the Duke of Harcourt said that empty space is perhaps the most important element of parks and gardens: it expresses the invisible, providing a hint of mystery and a center around which everything else revolves; it is the equivalent of a silent pause, which is an essential ingredient of eloquence.

The country road that runs along the west side of the lake, past the castle, leads to the entrance to San Liberato, which is marked by an imposing stone gateway; from here a drive winds its way through the natural vegetation, consisting of broom, rockroses, myrtles, and laurels, and then turns into an avenue lined with holm oaks and rosemary trimmed to form a hedge, amidst olive trees and large clumps of oleander.

garden covered with *Ceratostigma plumbaginoides*, valerian, capers, and small ferns. Beneath the arcaded portico is a collection of pelargoniums with scented leaves; a 'Cocktail' rose bush, a *Podranea ricasoliana* and a *Mandevilla laxa* (syn. *M. suaveolens*) climb the walls of the bell tower. On the right, behind the church, is an enchanting small garden created by Contessa Sanminiatelli in the shade of three large olive trees, where the dominant colors are gray, blue, and pink. It is reached by means of an archway flanked by a low wall, overhung with the long flowering branches of *Lespedesa thunbergii* (syn. *L. sieboldii*). The planting scheme here is highly sophisticated and the delicate colors blend in such a way that the notion of scale disappears in an overall impression of harmony. Japanese anemone, *Aster amellus*, *Leptospermum scoparium* 'Kiwi', *Pittosporum tenuifolium*, *Feijoa sellowiana*, *Ballota pseudodictamnus*, *Santolina chamaecyparissus*, *Lagerstroemia indica* 'Rosea', *Cistus ladanifer*, *Paeonia suffruticosa*, and *Felicia amelloides*, fill this romantic corner, which is intersected by a narrow path.

The avenue leads on past the church, flanked by screens of strawberry trees, laurels, myrtles, and mock privets (phyllyrea), to the circular piazza in front of the house, which is enclosed by a laurel hedge one and a half meters high and by holm oaks trimmed to a height of four meters or so to form a single belt of green. A large pine tree stands in the center like a host waiting to greet his guests. The piazza is ornamented with lemon trees in terracotta vases, and four pyramids of laurel mark the entrance to the villa, whose façade is completely covered by wisteria. The tall laurel hedge opens on to a vast green lawn which extends in front of the house and stretches away into the distance with the lake as a backdrop. The view, perfectly framed by groups of trees and unified by the wide green sweep of the grass, is a work of art, its sense of movement enhanced by the three different levels sloping down toward the lake.

The south-east wall of the house is entirely covered with *Trachelospermum jasminoides* and a 'Clair Matin' climbing rose, the fragrance of the first and the fine

The church, which is adorned with fifteenth-century frescoes and Roman relics, and approached by a portico of three arches surmounted by a loggia, stands in a small square dominated by a gigantic cypress with a fig tree at its side; on the right, surrounded by hedges of holm oak, are specimens of *Cycas revoluta*, *Callistemon viminalis*, and *Magnolia grandiflora*. Much of the façade of the church is covered by a pale pink *Rosa* 'Anemone' and a *Jasminum officinale*, while the wall below forms a miniature rock

BOTTOM: THE SPRING LEAVES OF A SCARLET OAK.
TOP: ONE OF THE MANY ROSE SPECIMENS IN THE GARDEN.
LEFT: THE VILLA "ISLAND OF ROSES" AND STEPS LEADING TO THE OPEN SPACE OF THE
VISTAS TOWARDS LAKE BRACCIANO.

ROSES WITH THE LONG GRAY HEDGE OF CARYOPTERIS.

quercifolia, and *Felicia amelloides*. Walking along paths strewn with rose petals through this profusion of scent and color is like entering a small flower-filled wood where the beauty derives not from isolated elements but from the relationship created between them.

This enchanting spot overflowing with flowers provides the perfect contrast to the still, gently sloping lawn where Conte Donato Sanminatelli began to plant his collection of trees in 1962. The first section is devoted to magnolias: *M. sargentiana robusta*, *M. × soulangiana* 'Alexandrina', and *M. grandiflora*. They are followed by a number of magnificent specimens of sweet gum (*Liquidambar styraciflua*), Caucasian fir (*Abies nordmanniana*), silver maple (*Acer saccharinum*), and *Cupressus cashmeriana*. The outer ring, formed by the great natural wood, is made up of chestnuts, field maples, and holm oaks. The collection continues with *Brachychiton acerifolius*, black gum (*Nyssa sylvatica*), another tulip tree, red oak, Japanese cherry (*Prunus* 'Takasago', syn. *P. sieboldii*), black walnut, and box elder (*Acer negundo* 'Variegatum').

The view back toward the house from the bottom of the garden includes a splendid group of Atlas cedars (*Cedrus atlantica*), with a well-defined copse of birches on

THE GRAY OF <u>CEDRUS ATLANTICA GLAUCA</u> AGAINST THE BLUE-GRAY OF THE HUGE OLIVE TREE.

blooms of the second making a scented wall of flowers which perfectly complements the beauty of the surrounding landscape. On the left a canopy, covered inside and out by *Parthenocissus tricuspidata* 'Veitchii', shelters azaleas, gardenias, camellias, and hydrangeas. The lawn extends as far as the swimming pool, which is concealed behind a laurel hedge about two meters high, linked to the house by a long hedge of 'Iceberg' roses: the white of the flowers stands out sharply against the green of the nearby wood.

At the beginning of this hedge, close to the house, stands a large tulip tree, which is covered with spectacular cream-colored flowers in the spring.

Across the lawn, enclosed by a ring of lavender, is an island of roses which must surely constitute one of the finest rose collections to be found in any Italian garden; the dense, vigorous bushes are cunningly interspersed with olive trees, lagerstroemia, and pomegranates, and on the outer edge, with *Crinum × powellii*, *Hydrangea*

THE PATHWAY AND GARDEN AT THE REAR OF THE CHURCH OF SAN LIBERATO.

the right. The lawn, which extends for about fifty meters, is bounded by a hedge of *Caryopteris* X *clandonensis* whose silver-gray contrasts sharply with the emerald green of the grass. This silver strip encloses a long bed of red, pink, and orange roses, bordered with gray stone, leaving a path down the center that leads to a circular fountain filled with water lilies. From the rose bed, steps lead to two upper levels covered with grass.

Donato Sanminiatelli was a great botanist, devoting much of his life to the creation of this garden and lavishing on it both his impeccable taste and the fruits of his extensive knowledge and humanistic culture: his gardening soul still lives on in the trees that he planted. Maria Odescalchi Sanminiatelli has continued her husband's work, determined to keep his memory alive through her loving care of their garden.

TOR SAN LORENZO

On the Pontine marshes a newly invented garden by Marchesa Lavinia Taverna Gallarati Scotti

"For me a garden was something that already existed, something that a house either did or did not have, like a billiard room." On the large and abandoned farm with its modest farmhouse that Marchese Federico Gallarati Scotti and his wife Donna Lavinia Taverna bought with great courage in 1956, there was neither billiard room nor garden, just some unfruitful land and the odd pine tree. The property lies a few kilometers from the sea, in the Pontine marshes, an area of great open, empty spaces to the south of Rome. "The last thing I had in mind when we came to live at Tor San Lorenzo was the creation of a garden and, to avoid the problem, I bought some very large umbrellas to provide shade at once without any complications."

ABOVE: THE GRAY, SKYBLUE, AND MAUVE ''ROOM'' SURROUNDED WITH OLIVE TREES.
RIGHT: OLD CLIMBING ROSE IN FLOWER AND COVERING THE VILLA.

Thirty years have gone by since that time, and, while there is still no billiard room at Tor San Lorenzo, the umbrellas have long since disappeared. Instead, there is a garden that has one of the richest varieties of botanical species in central Italy, as well as being one of the most elegant in its design.

In her book, *Un Giardino Mediterraneo*, Lavinia Gallarati Scotti Taverna tells the story of her garden, a garden described as if it were a royal court: new plants are welcomed with joy; flowers arrive from afar bearing great names and great promises; strangers are received and planted with diffidence but turn out to the "most loyal";

quiet shrubs suddenly "fall out of favor", and plants are abruptly "dismissed" or transferred with no other explanation than the temperament and the whims of a person who likes to describe herself as "a gardening bee". In fact, Lavinia Taverna's approach to gardening takes the form of an almost exclusive passion for the plants themselves; compositions and tonal harmonies take second place.

It was Russell Page who managed to convince her that true creativity lay in the design of the garden and that "there can be no beauty where everything is broken into pieces". So in 1967, the English landscape gardener was invited to "impose a structure on this disorder", and his

ABOVE: A NEW BORDER AT THE FRONT OF THE HOUSE WHICH IS BASED ON GRAY AND GRAY-GREEN FOLIAGE.
RIGHT: LAVANDULA STOECHAS, THRIFT AND DIANTHUS FORM PART OF A PURPLE-PINK BORDER.

designs still form the basic layout of the garden. It is made up of a succession of very large "rooms", each about 150 square meters in area, separated from one another by hedges of sweet bay (*Laurus nobilis*) and *Pittosporum tobira*. Naturally the plants that Russell Page originally intended for these rooms go on changing like the guests in a hotel. The one thing she was afraid of, Lavinia Taverna admits in her book, was "having to create a garden that could no longer be touched and that would have asked nothing from me but to be looked at."

The garden now covers almost six hectares, bordered by an artificial lake and by the large nursery of Tor San Lorenzo, which was set up by Marchesa Gallarati Scotti in partnership with other plantsmen and now offers one of the widest selections of typically Mediterranean plants in Italy, together with a great variety of camellias.

In the garden in front of the house, which greets the visitor to Tor San Lorenzo, the accent is on color, the delicate shades of the yellow-green leaves creating an infinitely subtle chromatic effect. Plants like *Gleditsia triacanthos inermis*, *Cestrum aurantiacum*, and *Griselinia littoralis* grow alongside *Abutilon striatum* 'Thomsonii', *Abutilon megapotanicum* 'Variegatum', and *Abutilon* 'Cloth of Gold', together with various types of euonymus, such as *Euonymus fortunei* and *E. fortunei* 'Emerald 'n' Gold'. These plants are all well suited to the nature of the soil in this location and hardy enough to withstand exposure to the wind.

A path runs away from the house to a pool filled with yellow waterlilies (*Nuphar lutea*) and Egyptian paper reeds (*Cyperus papyrus*); it marks the entrance to a long avenue of cypresses bordered by *Agapanthus* whose deep blue contrasts superbly with the dark green foliage of the trees. This avenue then leads on to two further rooms, one on either side of the path. In the first, Seville orange (*Citrus aurantium*) and *Myrtus Communis tarentina* trees pruned into spheres have been planted in a geometric pattern between hedges of *Pittosporum tobira*. In the room on the right, surrounded by large olives, the predominant colors are gray, sky-blue, mauve and yellow, and the

THE "ROOM" WITH SEVILLE ORANGES AND <u>MYRTUS</u> <u>COMMUNIS</u> <u>TARENTINA</u> PRUNED INTO SPHERES.

ZANTEDESCHIA AETHIOPICA AT THE LAKE'S EDGE.

various plants include common sage, *Ballota pseudo-dictamnus*, *Sorbaria aitchisonii*, *Alchemilla mollis*, *Artemisia absinthium*, rue, tulips, roses, various types of allium, long-spurred hybrid columbines, and *Hosta fortunei*. The walls of this room are formed by a hedge of *Camellia sasanqua*, whose flowers provide a kind of wallpaper decoration. All these plants have been chosen for the predominantly gray shades of their leaves or for their yellow or mauve flowers, which blend perfectly with the silvery leaves of the olives.

A broad and gently sloping path, bordered entirely by the silver-gray leaves and long white and mauve flower spikes of *Salvia leucantha*, leads to the white and lilac garden: here white tulips and 'Unique Blanche', 'Penelope', and 'Sea Foam' roses are mixed with *Libertia grandiflora*, *Gaura lindheimeri*, *Tulbaghia violacea*, *Iberis semperflorens*, *Lamium maculatum*, and white *Plumbago auriculata*. It is a perfect combination of plants in a delightfully subtle blend of colors; they have all been carefully chosen for their white or lilac flowers. It is of course Tor San Lorenzo's location, in an area of Lazio where the climate is particularly mild, that has made it possible to plant such delicate species.

A large space opens to the left of the path, planted with olives interspersed with large bushes of *Rosa* 'Mutabilis', whose colors change from pale pink to salmon and then to a darker pink: a carpet of small, deep blue *Iris histrioides* is spread beneath them, along with lesser periwinkle, bugle (*Ajuga reptans*), blue-eyed grass (*Sisyrinchium angustifolium*), and *Nandina domestica*. Here the olives give a distinctly Mediterranean character to the garden, and the bushes of rather informal pink roses are beautifully complemented by the intense blue of the ground cover plants beneath them.

To the right is the "Valley of Roses" where countless rose varieties, from Bourbon to cabbage roses (*Rosa* 'Centifolia Muscosa') and from Damask, to French roses, blend together in a deliberately uncoordinated range of colors. Lavinia Taverna's fancy takes an extravagantly romantic turn at this point: the valley turns down to the side of the lake where magnificent specimens of swamp cypress (*Taxodium distichum*) grow at the edge of the water, surrounded by water arums. Winding among the roses are various species of thyme (such as *Thymus serpyllum*, along with *Lavandula stoechas* and *Lavandula dentata*, *Pavonia intermedia rosea*, oleaster (*Elaeagnus angustifolia*), pinks, *Leptospermum scoparium*, and *Perovskia atriplicifolia*. The far end of the lake is enclosed by a high wall of eucalyptus that protects the garden from the north wind. A track leads uphill to a wood of common oaks (*Quercus robur*) and holm oaks, carpeted with *Viola cornuta*, Christmas roses, and acanthus (*Acanthus mollis*). The atmosphere in this area is completely different; it seems to me like another world, even though the connection with the rest of the garden is well established by the careful choice of plants. Here the shade provided by the trees, which have grown much more rapidly than normal owing to the humidity from the nearby lake, has created particularly favorable conditions for violets.

The route back towards the house passes through an area dedicated to shrubby veronicas (*Hebe salicifolia*), rockroses (*Cistus incanus*, *Cistus parviflorus*), and *Escallonia macrantha*, planted around small apple trees; ground cover

SWAMP CYPRESS (TAXODIUM DISTICHUM) IN THE LAKE.

is also provided by *Polygonum campanulatum*, which turns into a carpet of pink flowers from June to September. To the right is the "blue garden", where the plants are arranged in a precise geometric pattern: a basin containing blue waterlilies (*Nymphaea coerulea*) stands at its center, surrounded by four borders made up of various types of ceanothus, such as 'Trewithen Blue', *thyrsiflorus*, and 'Italian Skies', together with *Convolvulus mauritanicus*, *Plumbago Auriculata*, *Ceratostigma willmottianum*, *Solanum rantonnetii*, and *Sollya heterophylla*, whose different shades of blue blend with the light and dark green of the leaves. A little further on is the "Italian-style garden" whose geometric flowerbeds, bordered with sweet bay cut to a height of about thirty centimeters, are filled with white cushions of 'Sea Foam' and 'Swany' roses. The distinctive feature of these varieties is that their blooms are so densely packed that they cover the bed completely with a carpet of color.

The garden of Tor San Lorenzo is currently one of the most striking examples of the renaissance of the Italian garden, and a testimony to the botanical passion of its creator. Marchesa Gallarati Scotti Taverna can be regarded as one of the most outstanding representatives of that group of intelligent and imaginative gardeners who apply their great talents to the invention or reconstruction of their gardens.

VILLA POLISSENA

*The gardens of a royal residence
reflect the taste of the Twenties and of painter
Principe Enrico d'Assia*

When Mafalda of Savoy, the daughter of Victor Emanuel III, King of Italy, married Principe Filippo d'Assia in 1925, she received Villa Polissena as a wedding present from her father. The neoclassical house and its large park were separated by a wall from Villa Savoia, then the residence of the Italian royal family. The prince and princess enlarged the house, today the residence of their son, Principe Enrico d'Assia, and transformed the park which then consisted of uncultivated grassland and a few cypresses, into a garden that perfectly reflected the taste, culture, and fashions of the twenties. Cork oaks were brought from Sardinia, and pine trees were grown individually from seeds taken from the same pine cone; both the choice of the plants and the

ABOVE: THE CLASSICAL ITALIAN GARDEN FROM THE BALUSTRADE.
RIGHT: THE TRITON AND ITS POOL WITHIN THE CLASSICAL ITALIAN GARDEN.

design of the whole scheme were the work of Principe Filippo, who had studied architecture in Rome and applied to the garden not only his talent for scenography but also his cultural eclecticism, which embraced the art of Roman antiquity, the serene classicism of the Renaissance, and the exotic charms of the Japanese tradition. Out of the fusion of these elements was born the garden of Villa Polissena, whose composite and varied style is always kept in check by a predilection for the geometric and linear. Principe Enrico has devoted all his gardening skills to the maintenance of this balance: his talent as a painter is combined with his flair for theatrical design.

A pool was built at the side of the house in the thirties to house a fine statue of a Triton, the work of the school of Bernini, which the king had presented to his daughter. The pool was enclosed in the ordered charm of a classical Italian garden, surrounded by Roman busts that are now cloaked in ivy, and framed by a semicircle of tall cypresses. A long border of China roses (*Rosa* 'Mutabilis') runs along beneath the cypresses to a small patio adjoining the villa, where the walls are covered with *Plumbago auriculata* and varieties of clematis.

Three paths spread out like spokes from the front of the house, creating a perspective effect that gives the garden a sense of both depth and breadth. The central path is flanked by tall hedges of laurel and bordered by lilac and violet irises and pink oxalis; it directs the gaze towards a column topped by a statue of Hercules and, further on, a niche containing a Roman bust.

Concealed at the end of the second path is what is perhaps the prince's most precious creation: a small Pompeiian garden that is an exact copy, in its measurements and design, of a real garden in Pompeii. What underlies its conception is not so much an interest in archeology as a purely esthetic desire to recreate the lost patrician calm of the original Roman garden on which it is based. It is planted with olives, roses, and small carnations; ivy covers the low walls, and a sheet of water in a rectangular pool is highlighted by the flowers of white water lilies.

A JAPANESE MAPLE ACER PALMATUM ATOP A SMALL MOUND.

The third path leads through a pergola of purple wisteria, whose flowers mingle with those of a white variety that has climbed to the top of a nearby oak tree; the path then runs on toward a small lake, which is covered with water lilies and surrounded by a Japanese garden. It cannot really be said that this garden reflects the true Oriental style but it reproduces the image of it that had been spread by the vogue for the exotic at the end of the nineteenth century, which also inspired the decoration of a drawing room in the villa. The serpentine lake is surrounded by maples of various shades and species, together with both herbaceous and tree peonies, Japanese iris (*Iris ensata*, syn. *I. kaempferi*), *Iris pseudacorus*, azaleas, camellias, columbines (a flower much loved by Principessa Mafalda), mimosas, bamboos, and a fine Judas tree (*Cercis siliquastrum*), all illuminated by a Chinese lantern. A bamboo brake opens out near a gate leading to Villa Savoia.

The great park that surrounds the gardens extends for almost two hectares and is planted with majestic pines, large clumps of golden broom, small palms (*Chamaerops humilis*), laurels, and a fine cedar of Lebanon. Overall, the atmopshere is that of a purely Mediterranean garden, such as Principe Enrico d'Assia depicts in his paintings, which are dotted with cypresses and Roman statues in the neoclassical style. And it is here that the garden as a form of artistic expression comes together with the representations of it in the prince's pictures, which reflect the image he carries within him of the place where he grew up and the spirit of the garden created by his father.

The eclectic, cosmopolitan taste, based on a love of the remote and the ancient, that produced the garden has given it a style that gains in variety what it may have lost in depth. The classical, Pompeiian, and Japanese gardens, laid out according to a strictly disciplined linear design, are like garden pictures that mirror the taste both of the twenties and of the late nineteenth century, the belle epoque, which was enthralled by *Madam Butterfly*, loved open-air theaters, and delighted in composing sentimental *tableaux vivants* in romantically beautiful gardens.

BOTTOM: THE STATUE OF HERCULES ON ITS COLUMN HIGH IN THE CORK OAKS.
TOP: A ROMAN BUST PEERS OVER THE BALCONY TOWARDS THE MAIN PART OF THE GARDEN.
RIGHT: ONE OF THE THREE PATHS LEADING ALONG LAUREL HEDGES TOWARDS A ROMAN STATUE.

ABOVE: BAMBOOS FORM A "BRAKE" TO A GATE.
RIGHT: A STATUE AT THE EDGE OF THE JAPANESE GARDEN.
FAR RIGHT: THE JAPANESE GARDEN, WITH LANTERN
IRISES AND NYMPHEA IN THE POOL.

ISOLA BISENTINA

On a small island on Lake Bolsena an overgrown natural garden is restored by architect and painter Principe Giovanni Del Drago

"Oh longed-for green solitude far from the sound of men": Gabriele D'Annunzio's words seem to have been written specifically to describe Isola Bisentina in Lake Bolsena, which is undoubtedly one of the most magical and fascinating places in Italy. Its name derives from nearby "Visentium", a ruined Etruscan city that once stood on the shore of the lake. The island is seven hundred meters long, five hundred meters wide and two kilometers in circumference, making up a total area of seventeen hectares, part woods, part pasture, and part garden. Cliffs rise sheer out of the lake on its northern and eastern sides, with Monte Tabor, completely encircled by ancient holm oaks and common oaks, at the centre. On the level land below it stands the

ABOVE: ONE OF THE CHAPELS HIGH ABOVE THE ETRUSCAN COLOMBARIUM (PIGEON COOP) OVERLOOKING LAKE BOLSENA.
LEFT: COSMOS BIPINNATUS 'SENSATION'.

THE VIEW ALONG THE ITALIAN-STYLE GARDEN.

principal church, designed by Vignola, with an adjoining monastery set in a large garden, and a harbor surrounded by dense greenery.

When the Saracens began their raids on the coastal regions of the Maremma, the flat marshlands of southern Tuscany, in the ninth century, people living in towns near the sea decided to take permanent refuge on the island, setting up an autonomous community. The island was inhabited until the eleventh century, when the Saracen invasions came to an end. By then, powerful families had set their sights on it, going so far as to burn down the inhabitants' houses, with the result that, little by little,

the place was abandoned. All that remained intact were the Rocca, or fortress, with a garrison of men-at-arms, and the parish church. Then, at the behest of Pope Urban IV, the island was turned into a notorious prison where churchmen guilty of heresy or serious crimes were held for life. The prison-pit is still clearly visible today, excavated out of the hill of tufa, with a cylindrical cell at a depth of twenty meters. In 1431, Pope Eugene IV granted the island to the Observant Friars Minor, to build a monastery and a new church. Ranuccio III Farnese chose to be buried in the church because of the serenity of its atmosphere and the incomparable beauty of its site,

160

THE CLOISTER AND LAWNS.

shaded by majestic holm oaks. From that time on, the Farnese family brought luster to Isola Bisentina, over the centuries commissioning the most famous architects of the age to build a church and six chapels, which are scattered over the island in extremely beautiful locations. The place was visited by Pope Pius II in 1462 and, in memory of this event, he left instructions that another small church should be built on the summit of Monte Tabor. The main church was rebuilt by Vignola towards the middle of the sixteenth century, while one of the chapels is the work of Antonio Sangallo the younger, tiny and charming in the grace and purity of its lines.

In 1870, after many changes of fortune, the island eventually passed out of the church's control and into private hands. As well as offering hospitality to a number of popes, it had received, in 1719, a visit from the Old Pretender, James Edward Stuart, and his wife, Clementina Sobieski.

This brief outline of the island's history shows that Isola Bisentina has often seen bloody and cruel times. Though it is peaceful today, perhaps its adversities have not been entirely forgotten: a tunnel of oleanders leads to the landing stage on the shore where, immersed in the greenery of water-loving plants and surrounded by great

HUNDREDS OF FROGS HAVE MADE THEIR HOMES IN THE GARDEN POOLS.

pots of blue hydrangeas, two enigmatic stone sphinxes seem to offer silent testimony to the past.

In 1912, the island was bought by Principessa Beatrice Potenziani del Drago, wife of the Duca di Roccapiemonte Ravaschieri-Fieschi; the duke was the model for the character of Sperelli in the novel *Il piacere* (Pleasure) by his friend Gabriele D'Annunzio. Today it belongs to Principessa Ornella Ravaschieri-Fieschi, the aunt of Principe Giovanni del Drago, an architect and painter, who in 1986 started the work of restoration of the monastery and garden that is currently under way. His aim is to recreate the natural garden and the Italian-style garden, both of which had been totally devoured by the island's natural vegetation. He began by cutting down the spontaneous growth that had choked every prospect, cleared a wide grass-covered avenue in front of the church, and restored to their former glory the stately olives, holm and common oaks, alders, and laurels. This long and spacious avenue leads to the shore of the lake, where the image of Vignola's cupola is reflected in the water. Beneath the great trees a collection of hydrangeas grouped into different species, such as *H. anomala petiolaris, aspera*, sargentiana, *quercifolia, paniculata, macrophylla*, and *arborescens*, adds a delicate haze of color to the landscape. On the right a ring of alders forms a circular chamber.

Alongside the right-hand wall of the church, which is largely covered by a *Macfadyena unguis-cati* and a purple *Parthenocissus tricuspidata* 'Veitchii', the prince has designed an Italian-style garden inspired by Giusto Utens' famous lunettes of 1598, now in the Museo Topografico in Florence. It is divided into three parts, with seasonal flower beds bordered by yew and box hedges and a parterre to complement the severe and imposing lines of the church. On the left stands the cloister of the monastery, an enormous wisteria partly covering its lofty wrought-iron roof: it overlooks a large olive grove which stretches away beneath, the silvery leaves of its ancient trees seeming to reflect the waters of the lake.

Along the shoreline are magnificent old holm oaks which have seeded themselves naturally, forming a dense and rather mysterious wood. On the slopes of Monte Tabor the dense growth is broken every so often by a chapel, sheltered and almost hidden by the greenery that surrounds it, heightening the impression that the island is cut off from the world, part of antiquity or somehow suspended in time. The view from the top of the mountain is incomparable: the whole lake is spread out below, its water so perfectly transparent that it is possible to see Etruscan sarcophagi resting on the bottom.

Around the monastery are pleasant meadows ringed by oaks and pines, and a small garden reminiscent of the

THE OLIVE GROVE THAT IS ALLOWED A COMPLETE NATURAL CYCLE.

VIGNOLA'S CHURCH DOMINATES THE NEWLY RE-CREATED ITALIAN-STYLE GARDEN.

style of art nouveau, with flowerbeds outlined with *Abelia* x *grandiflora* and parterres of seasonal flowers, ferns, and a few palms.

The island owes its great beauty both to its indigenous holm and common oaks, laurels and alders, all legendary trees redolent of ancient myth and magic, and to the species that have been planted by man – the olives and flowering plants – which have been introduced in such a way that they appear completely natural. The Principe del Drago has enhanced the charm of the place by creating light-filled gaps, judiciously cutting down trees to open up "telescopic views" that sweep from one part of the lake to another. This allows beams of light, accompanied by reflections from the lake, to break

through the greenery, highlighting different areas of the garden at different times of day: at dawn and sunset it is spellbindingly beautiful.

The work that the prince has carried out himself, assisted only by the men working on the restoration of the monastery, is an indication of the passion that he has always felt for plants and of the courage that has inspired him. In restoring Isola Bisentina he has succeeded in bringing back to life one of the most magical natural gardens in Italy.

An inscription over the entrance to the monastery, attributed to Gabriele D'Annunzio, reads: "It may be that one day I shall carry my spirit to this place, out of the storm . . .".

IL CANILE

*White terraces on the island of
Capri "dressed" in exotic colors by costume
designer Umberto Tirelli*

A passion for plants can lead people down some strange paths; it can even cause them to bring a pine tree into the bedroom that is so big it goes right through the ceiling to the floor above ... This is what has happened at Umberto Tirelli's house at Punta Tragara on the island of Capri.

For over thirty years Tirelli has worked as a costume designer for the theater, the ballet, the opera, and the cinema, both on faithful historical reconstructions and on inventive new productions. A friend of Luchino Visconti and Franco Zeffirelli, and creator of the costumes for *Amadeus*, his work in the theater has taken him all over the globe; as a result he has been able to assemble one of the most important costume collections in the world,

ABOVE: BOUGAINVILLEA JUTTING OUT OF THE ROCK FACE.
LEFT: THE MAIN TERRACE ALONGSIDE THE VILLA.

and has recently donated it to the city of Florence, which he regards as the symbol of a perfect marriage between craftsmanship and art. The items in this wonderful collection cover a period of nearly three hundred years, from 1700 to 1970.

Tirelli has a passion for flowers, a passion which he felt a great need to indulge when, in 1968, he and the music festival director Dino Trappetti bought a piece of land on Capri. On it stood a country cottage called "Il Canile", set amid vineyards, olives, and orange and lemon trees. At the beginning of the century the property was owned by Conte Vismara, who used it to raise Neapolitan mastiffs: hence the name "Il Canile", which means "The Kennel". The house overlooks a reservoir which very probably dates back to the reign of the Roman Emperor Tiberius, and it looks out almost directly over the famous Faraglioni rocks: the view from its garden terrace is one of the most spectacular that I have ever seen. It was graphically described by the traveler Conte Gastone della Torre Rezzonico in 1794:

"The ninth villa of Tiberius is set at Tragara, which forms the last promontory of the island, to the southeast of that of the Certosa. There used to be a sort of harbor here, and it is thought that Tiberius used it for a fleet of armed vessels for his defense. A few remains of hydraulic constructions are still visible, perfectly preserved in spite of the violence of the sea, which holds great sway here. A magnificent aqueduct, that winds around, and many ruins of ancient dwellings with garden parterres . . . .".

Even today the promontory of Tragara is virtually unspoiled, and the area is rich in wild flowers, including twenty species of orchid and fifteen of dog rose.

ABOVE LEFT: A PINK BOUGAINVILLEA GROWING ON THE SIDE OF THE VILLA.
ABOVE RIGHT: ONE OF THE HUNDREDS OF CHINESE HIBISCUS ON THE UPPER PATIO.
RIGHT: BOUGAINVILLEA CREEPING OVER THE UPPER PATIO.

When Umberto Tirelli began work on his garden, he decided to lay it out as a series of terraces, linked together laterally by flights of steps. From the entrance gate, steps lead up to the first terrace, to a long pergola entirely covered with a colorful range of bougainvilleas; along its outer border are roses, Chinese hibiscus (*Hibiscus rosa-sinensis*), and *Plumbago auriculata*, while the beautiful dark green leaves of marsh marigold (*Caltha palustris*) extend along the shady inner border, contrasting effectively with the brightly-colored bougainvillea roof. The view from the wooden bench in the center of the pergola includes not only this cascade of flowers in shades of red, yellow and purple but also, in the words of Neapolitan novelist and botanist Edwin Cerio, "the sky carved from a solid block of cobalt, the sea all crystals of copper sulfate".

The second terrace, sheltered by a high wall of rock entirely covered by a white bougainvillea, is bordered by various types of pelargonium with scented leaves, rosemary, heliotrope, and *Datura ceratocaula*, and ornamented with lemon and grapefruit trees in terracotta vases.

When the lemon trees are in bloom, the air here is fragrant with their blossom, mixed intoxicatingly with the scents rising from the sea. White *Trachelospermum jasminoides*, geraniums, and hydrangeas, melting into a cascade of white bougainvillea, soften the harsh rocks of Capri which enclose the house and make such a theatrical backdrop to the garden. Vases of white and blue pottery, and clouds of white hydrangeas decorate both the living room and the terrace in front so that the house and garden seem to be inseparable from each other and from their typically Mediterranean setting.

On the third terrace a large collection of single- and double-flowered Chinese hibiscus make a colorful display during the summer months; one plant actually has three different grafts, of white, yellow, and pink flowers. Each level of the garden has its own distinct perfumes, and here the air is scented by *Cestrum nocturnum*, which is planted along the sides of the terrace.

Higher still, a thicket of *Colocasia esculenta antiquorum* grows in the shade of a large olive tree, enlivening the

BOTTOM: WHITE BOUGAINVILLEA ALONG THE HIGH WALL OF ROCK OF THE SECOND TERRACE.
TOP: A SIDE VIEW ALONG THE ROCK FACE SHOWING THE LUXURIANT GROWTH OF BOUGAINVILLEA.

THE FARAGLIONI ROCKS AND COBALT BLUE SEA BEYOND THE SHARP OUTLINES OF CORDYLINES.

gray rock with its broad, glossy leaves. A charming collection of fuchsias and begonias hangs from the branches of the tree in little moss-lined iron baskets, which sway in the wind over a sea of hydrangeas, ferns, and impatiens, like a multi-colored costume fluttering in the breeze.

Pots of white geraniums and hibiscus decorate the terrace in front of the bedrooms, where the walls are covered with bougainvillea, *Podranea ricasoliana*, and *Jasminum sambac*, and a small area is set aside for antique white roses that open like enormous butterflies.

On the roof terrace is a delightful nursery in miniature, where the gardener, Costanzo, painstakingly prepares seedlings for summer flowering. There is also a small container garden for vegetables and herbs, especially basil, which is grown from seeds brought from all over the world. This unusual roof garden is framed by trees and shrubs typical of Capri – mastic, carob, and strawberry trees, cypresses, oaks, and junipers, brooms and laurels – while the mountain above, which forms a natural amphitheater, protects the more delicate species.

Edwin Cerio has said that Capri is too beautiful to be dressed up. But Umberto Tirelli has succeeded in dressing his garden to suit the character of the island, decorating it with vivid color and filling it with scent, so that Capri's beauty is heightened rather than diminished and its drama made all the more compelling.

LA MORTELLA

On the volcanic island of Ischia the luxuriant rock garden created by Lady Susan Walton

"I am Nestor's cup / and whoever drinks from this cup / will be assailed by the subtle and seductive / charm of Aphrodite of the beautiful crown." These verses are engraved on a cup from the eighth century BC found during excavation of the necropolis of Monte Vico, which dominates the promontory at the northern tip of the island of Ischia.

It is easy to understand why this island in the Bay of Naples exerted such a hold on the imagination of the great English composer Sir William Walton. In 1950, he drove down to Forio in a Bentley with his young Argentinian wife, Lady Susana, intending to stay for six months, and remained there until 1983, the year in which he died.

ABOVE: WILLIAM'S ROCK WHICH OVERLOOKS FORIO.
RIGHT: THE VIEW TOWARDS THE HOUSE FROM THE LOWER END OF THE MAIN POOL.

At that time, not long after the War, the island was visited by few people, and scarcely any foreigners, and Sir William Walton found there the peace and serenity that would allow him to work on his music without interruption. Lady Walton was a true pioneer, having to adjust, in the early days, to a tough way of life: the house they rented was dilapidated; there was no water and an unpredictable electricity supply, and they were surrounded by curious locals who regarded them as eccentrics. For many years they shuttled back and forth between London and Ischia, remaining on the island for long periods, especially in the winter. Eventually, they decided to buy a plot of land on which to build their own house, and Lady Walton describes how the site was chosen in her book of memoirs, *William Walton – Behind the Façade*, published by Oxford University Press in 1988:

"When William was busy composing the Second Symphony, I resolved to find a place of our own on Ischia. Forio seemed an ideal place for William to work. Behind Casa Cirillo a road had been cut through the vineyards, allowing access to the hill beyond. The evergreen ilex covered the steep slope, and enormous boulders made the area quite dramatic. Our friends the Casatis had already bought one part, and I fell in love with the adjoining land. Both Larry and William were of the opinion that I was crazy, because the land was nothing but a stone quarry and buying it would mean spending the rest of our lives breaking stones. However, William came round to admiring the immense lava boulders which loomed over the long valley, well defended from the sea-winds. After inspecting it several times, he agreed to buy it."

And thus was born "La Mortella", as the house was called after the local name given to the common myrtle, which grows wild in that part of the island.

The basic design for the rock garden came from the landscape architect Russell Page, who advised Lady

THE MAIN POOL VIEWED FROM THE BALCONY OF "LA MORTELLA".

THE AUSTRALIAN TREE FERN OVERSHADOWS A HUGE EXPANSE OF FUCHSIAS.

Walton to build straight dry-stone walls to contain the soil of the hillside, to clear away the vegetation that covered the larger boulders in order to create a contrast with the trees – which were planted as very young saplings so that their roots could gain a good hold on the ground – and always to plant hundreds of plants of the same species rather than just one.

The work of clearing the hill, constructing the terraces, and getting the plants to settle in took seven years. Russell Page came back after ten years and designed a series of fountains, which run along the central axis of the L-shaped garden, with one last fountain set at the end of its shorter arm. He suggested Lady Walton should plant a variety of Mexican species on the terrace below the house, to surround the Australian tree ferns (*Cyathea medullaris*) and the *Metrosideros excelsa* trees. On yet another visit, he designed the octagonal gray stone fountain in honor of Sir William Walton's eightieth birthday.

Lady Walton devoted herself enthusiastically to the creation of her garden, growing trees and shrubs from

LANTANA MONTEVIDENSIS ALONG A WALL WITH RUSELIA EQUISETIFORMIS (R. JUNCEA) BELOW.

seeds brought from all over the world. She began with the trees she remembered from her childhood, such as *Jacaranda mimosifolia*, Judas trees, magnolias, *Chorisia speciosa*, and *Eucalyptus ficifolia*. The remains of the lava flows from the old volcano lay at the bottom of the valley and Lady Walton had the brilliant idea of dumping all the waste from the garden there, which produced excellent humus. She planted great laurel hedges, to provide protection from the harsh wind known as the sirocco, and a wide variety of local species, blending them skillfully with tropical and subtropical plants such as the famous black-trunked ferns that her husband brought back from Australia. At the top of the hill two enormous cisterns were dug to hold water, since many species, especially the subtropical varieties, required constant irrigation.

Sir William and Lady Walton had come to know Ischia very well during their early stays on the island, and in long walks over Monte Epomeo they had discovered several rare species of ferns (*Woodwardia radicans*), cyclamens, wild violets, and other plants that grew only in that area and that they subsequently transplanted to "La Mortella".

The house was built in the lee of the mountain, facing south and therefore filled with light; the windows and doors are framed with blocks of lava, and the house itself, in local granite, blends perfectly with its natural surroundings – with the olives, tall gray palms (*Brahea armata*), silver-leaved cypresses (*Cupressus glabra* 'conica'), and silver-gray rocks that enclose it.

Today, "La Mortella" is largely an exotic rock garden, designed on the basis of a perfect balance of "shade, sun, and seclusion". Whenever I go, I like to begin a tour of the garden at the end of the long arm of the L: at the center of the first fountain is a gray rock surmounted by a basin, with a wide variety of plants set around it, forming a small circular garden: camellias, *Senecio bicolor cineraria*, *Fuchsia magellanica*, wormwood (*Artemisia absinthium*), myrtle, *Plumbago auriculata*, columbines, and *Achimenes longiflora*. This area is enclosed by an espalier of *Camellia sasanqua* and *Camellia japonica* bordered by *Bergenia cordifolia*. A small path leads to the left, where groups of camellias, again planted among the gray rocks, with begonias at their base, are strikingly effective; at the end of the path are the huge green umbrellas of the famous Australian ferns *Cyathea medullaris*, which are not only a great rarity but are also one of the garden's most distinctive features.

Down a few steps, among camellias growing in the

AGAPANTHUS LILLIES AT THE END OF THE GARDEN.

running almost the whole length of the garden, interrupted only by three tall jets of water. I find the views in the direction of the house magical: the profusion of brightly-colored tropical plants, the strong light, the scents, the deep shadows, and the ever-present murmur of running water all combine to call to mind the exotic delights of an Arab garden.

The narrow strip of water draws a dividing line between sections of plants chosen for their color: in the background is the blue valley filled with hydrangeas, African lilies, violets, and Brunfelsia; to the right, a yellow area, planted with day lilies, *Hedychium gardnerianum*, Chinese hibiscus, and *Lantana camara*; on the left, the pink section, with azaleas, hydrangeas, daturas, and *Raphiolepsis indica*.

The third, octagonal, fountain – again set along the line of the channel – is bordered by columbines, *Viburnum plicatum*, *Geranium palmatum*, *Carissa grandiflora*, veronicas, gardenias, and azaleas.

A wide expanse of colorful flowering plants extends in the direction of the great central fountain, with its oval pool, which is set at a slightly higher level, at the foot of the house. Huge lava boulders emerge like sea monsters from the water, among lilies and lotuses, paper reeds, wisteria, myrtles, and mastic trees, sprayed by a tall jet of water that rises from the center. The large basin is completely surrounded by a tropical garden of great gray palms (*Brahea armata*), *Yucca elephantipes*, *Puya raimondii*, *Agave ferox*, *Euphorbia candelabrum*, *Cordyline indivisa*, and *Aloe arborescens*; the dry-stone walls beneath are covered with *Russelia equisetiformis*, valerian, and *Lantana montevidensis*. All around are tall trees such as *Jacaranda mimosifolia*, *Callistemon viminalis*, and *Metrosideros excelsa*. The trunk of an enormous dead cypress has been completely overgrown by *Thunbergia alata*, like a tall obelisk decorated with lilac butterflies.

A semicircular flight of steps leads up towards the house, framed by two ivy-covered sphinxes and adorned with *Cycas revoluta*. At the end of the rock garden is a single specimen of *Arbutus andrachne*, which stands at the

YUCCAS IN FLOWER.

shade of tulip trees, ferns, *Amaryllis belladonna*, *Monstera deliciosa*, and hydrangeas, stands a large *Chorisia speciosa* tree surrounded by *Magnolia grandiflora*, *Magnolia stellata*, gardenias, *Jasminum sambac*, *Agapanthus africanus*, *Strelitzia reginae*, and *Polygala myrtifolia*. Beyond is the second, circular fountain, fed by the long, narrow channel of water that links them all. Semi-aquatic plants such as water arums encircle the fountain, and a straight stone path leads to a bench in a peaceful corner enclosed by pale pink *Brugmansia* x *insignis*, *Chamaedorea elegans*, pink *Lantana sellowiana*, and in the background an *Erythrina speciosa*. From here the gray stone water channel can be seen

NYMPHEAS, ROCKS OF LAVA AND A FOUR-METER PLUME OF WATER ARE THE MAIN FEATURES OF THE OVAL POOL.

entrance to the villa; at Christmas time it is covered with white flowers, which contrast strikingly with the deep red of its trunk.

A drive slopes gently downwards to lead out of the garden, and a path on the left climbs the rock to the terraces above, planted with the yellow-flowered *Lantana camara*, *Senecio bicolor cineraria*, broom, a number of large cypresses and magnolias, *Echium fastuosum*, and strawberry trees. At the top stands a small greenhouse used for the propagation of the more delicate species by the expert gardener, Maria Esposito, who has cared for the garden for many years.

The drive descends further, flanked by grapefruit trees, to the boundary of the garden, where coral trees (*Erythrina crista-galli*) and *Erythrina speciosa*, African lilies, fuchsias, *Amaryllis belladonna*, and wayfaring bushes (*Lantana camara*) are enclosed by a large laurel hedge.

In what was described at the time as "nothing but a stone quarry", Lady Walton has succeeded in creating one of the most unusual and spectacular tropical gardens to be found anywhere: an exotic, luxuriant garden that reflects a spirit as strong and implacable as the rocks that surround it, a garden that has prevailed triumphantly over Ischia's arid, inhospitable terrain.

LO STUDIO

Leonardo and Katherine Mondadori recreate a small perfumed paradise on the most beautiful island in the world

"So after the world had finally been set in order, over the course of the centuries, the botanical habitat of Capri was formed and the most beautiful, the richest Flora in existence took up permanent residence there." Thus wrote Edwin Cerio in his book *Flora privata di Capri*; he was born on the island in 1875 to an Irish mother and a Neapolitan father, and died there in 1960, having made his permanent home there in the 1920s. He had a passionate love of the local flora, and devoted his life to the study of the island's botany, paleontology, and zoology. A naturalist, photographer, and artist, he was one of the great personalities of Capri during its golden age. He built villas and laid out gardens that are among the finest on the island, and in 1911 he

ABOVE: THE GATEWAY TO THE PROPERTY COVERED WITH BOUGAINVILLEA.
LEFT: THE SMALL COURTYARD AND POOL WHICH GIVES A MOORISH AIR TO THE ENTRANCE AREA.

ABOVE: THE TOP TERRACE WITH ITS VIEW ACROSS CAPRI TO ANACAPRI.
LEFT: THE WEST-FACING PART OF THE HOUSE

chose an idyllic position on Via Tragara, one of Capri's most scenic points, for Lo Studio.

In 1986, Leonardo Mondadori, a member of the great family of Milanese publishers, was fascinated by this earthly paradise, and he decided to buy the place. The garden had by then fallen into such decay that little or nothing remained of its original beauty, and much work had to be done to recreate it.

The garden consists of three terraces, linked together by small flights of steps, and, like almost all the gardens on the island, it is carved out of the rock. Narrow steps, enclosed by high walls covered with *Tecomaria capensis* and *Macfadyena unguis-cati*, climb up to the first level, where the air is filled with the extraordinary scent of the *Carissa grandiflora* 'Prostrata' that grows along the top of the steps. A group of large lemon trees, carpeted underfoot with cotton lavender (*Santolina chamaecyparissus*) and *Lavandula angustifolia*, extends as far as the swimming pool area, whose entrance is marked by a gigantic cypress, a symbol of eternity; in the right-hand corner the leafy branches of a mulberry tree make a pool of shade. Dark purple bougainvillea and *Jasminum officinale* grow along the arches that enclose the swimming pool, which is like an open-air living room, decorated with vases of

PANSIES ADDING COLOR TO A SMALL AREA OF HERB GARDEN.

Chinese hibiscus (*Hibiscus rosa-sinensis*); two splendid specimens of *Ficus lyrata* stand in pots at the side, and in one corner is a *Cestrum nocturnum* in a large oil jar; its flowers give off a strong sweet scent that permeates the whole of the garden. The outer wall enclosing the pool is formed by espaliered lemon trees bordered by milkweed (*Asclepias curassavica*), *Brugmansia suaveolens*, and *Carissa grandiflora*. Above the arches, two large concrete containers have been used to make a kitchen garden, where all the vegetables for the house are grown – tomatoes, eggplants, capsicums, and a variety of salad greens; on their outer side the containers are bordered by *Santolina chamaecyparissus*, rosemary, and rose scented geranium, and the pergola that covers them is festooned with clusters of lilac-colored *Solanum wendlandii* and the long branches of *Podranea ricasoliana* which are studded with pink flowers.

The second level is marked by another tall cypress whose crown reaches to the height of the top terrace; a small herb garden has been laid out around a basin of water lilies, and perhaps an attempt has been made here to recreate a passage of Edwin Cerio's book:

"But the wild plants at once regain the upper hand, rivaling one another to produce the strongest scent: the round-leaved mint (*Mentha rotundifolia*) and penny royal (*Mentha pulegium*) intone a duet of fragrances, and in the more remote places their perfumed refrain is joined by the oregano (*Origanum vulgare* 'Viride') which is overcome with longing for its cousin, the sweet marjoram (*Origanum majorana*) . . .".

The wild plants of Capri are supplemented here with thyme, cotton lavender, rosemary, lavender, *Cistus ladanifer*, veronica, *Abelia chinensis*, and *Aloysia triphylla*, while another section of the terrace is given over to *Jacaranda mimosifolia*, *Strelitzia nicolai*, and *Bauhinia variegata* 'Candida', surrounded by large pots of *Camellia japonica* and *Echium fastuosum*. Succulent grapefruits ripen on a tree right in front of the lower floor of the house, while the wall of the staircase leading to the third level is covered with caper plants and bougainvillea.

An enormous oil jar filled with *Trachelospermum jasminoides* invites one to climb up to the entrance to the Studio, whose façade is adorned with an old Spanish portal and framed by purple bougainvillea, lemon trees and cypresses. There is a faintly Moorish air about the small courtyard here; on the left is a rectangular basin filled with water lilies and Egyptian paper reeds and surrounded by pots of begonias and hydrangeas. Screening a row of cypresses in front is a wall with caper bushes sprouting from between its stones and *Abelia chinensis*, Rugosa roses, and holly growing along its base. On the rear wall, large specimens of *Camellia japonica* are shaded from the sun by a small copse of holm oaks planted at a slightly lower level; the undergrowth consists of *Pittosporum tobira*, *Clivia miniata*, and a variety of other shrubs. A small path leads up from this point to the level of the vegetable garden.

The terrace to the right of the house is covered with a mass of purple bougainvillea and dotted with large vases of dark pink Chinese hibiscus; *Jasminum officianale affine* and *Jasminum officianale* planted in oil jars climb the walls. This magical area remains one of D'Annunzio's words: "All at once the jasmine seemed to give off a stronger scent, as if a heart had begun to beat faster." The terrace extends right round the house, the scents of gardenias,

THE SWIMMING POOL WITH DARK PURPLE BOUGAINVILLEA AND GRAPE VINES
GROWING ALONG THE ARCHES.

jasmine, *Stephanotis floribunda*, and *Cestrum nocturnum* drifting through the air in the evening, as if each were trying to outdo the other.

At the back of the house, across a small terraced garden, another flight of steps leads up to the top terrace, where large vases of *Datura metel* 'Aurea' and pillars of jasmine frame a superb view of Capri, the "essential island and receptacle of all Mediterranean species", to use Edwin Cerio's words.

Leonardo Mondadori began the work of restoring this remarkable property in 1986, and in the space of a few short years he has brought it back to life. Helped by the landscape architect Marco Mosterts, who has interpreted the spirit of Lo Studio with great sensitivity and care in his choice of plants, he has inbred the place with a part of himself that has fused and blended with the remains of the original garden, which was so much loved by its former owner.

IL BIVIERE

The Mediterranean garden of Principe and Principessa Scipione Borghese in the sun-drenched land where lemon trees flower

"Where the lemon trees flower and golden oranges glitter amidst the brown foliage": these famous words were used by Goethe to describe Sicily in his *Italian Journey*, and they perfectly convey the character of the countryside around Catania in which Il Biviere is set, a sun-drenched deserted landscape of citrus plantations and fields of grain.

The Lentini estate has been owned by the family of Principe and Principessa Scipione Borghese Branciforte Trabia since 1300, and it extends over an area of land, reclaimed in 1800, that once consisted of lakes and marsh. Part of it had originally been occupied by two lakes, the waters of Lake Biviere, which covered 1,200 hectares, flowing into Lake Ercole, where

ABOVE: THE CHAPEL S.ANDREA AND ELEVATED "WALL" OF SUCCULENTS AND CACTI WHICH RUNS
ALONG THE LENGTH OF THE ENTRANCE DRIVE.
RIGHT: THE OLD WHARF WITH A COLLECTION OF CACTI.

PARKINSONIA ACULEATA

A MAGNIFICENT SPECIMEN OF OREOCEREUS CELSIANUS.

local inhabitants fished as the ancient Phoenicians had done, taking advantage of the west wind that drove fish along with the current into the lake. In 1692, an earthquake caused both lakes to disappear, but the wharfs of the harbor, which are connected to an austerely simple building once used by the fishing industry, and the old chapel of San Andrea alongside it, have survived intact.

In 1968, Principe and Principessa Borghese decided to make this property their home: the land was uncultivated, without even a single tree, but their passion for plants drove them to create what is today a rare and splendid Mediterranean garden, covering some three and a half hectares, whose most distinctive feature is a magnificent collection of succulents. The princess has gathered specimens from all over the world, and has turned the old wharf on the banks of the lake into a fascinating Botanical garden. It is remarkable to see so many rare species in a private garden, and especially to

find them so well documented: they have all been catalogued according to their year of planting and place of origin. The rarities include *Agave americana* 'Medio-picts Alba', *Agave attenuata*, *Yucca elephantipes*, *Cochal opuntia robusta*, *Aloe marlothii*, *Myrtillo cactus*, *Agave fourcroydes*, *Aloe commutata* and *Yucca aloifolia* 'Marginata'. The agaves in this collection have grown to enormous size and have taken on monstrous shapes in the heat and humidity of the local climate: according to the princess, succulents need a lot of water to produce such results.

In front of the house are honey locust trees (*Gleditsia triacanthos*), which grow as well here as they do in their native land of Sicily, together with *Jacaranda mimosifolia*, and *Xanthorrhoea arborea* which flowers from June onwards. Four large grapefruit trees (*Citrus* x *paradisi*) on the terrace adorn the entrance to the house and fill the whole garden with the scent of their flowers.

At the foot of a flight of stone steps to the left of the

house – which is completely covered on this side by bougainvillea and framed by a *Jacaranda mimosifolia* – stands a magnificent specimen of *Parkinsonia aculeata* which I always admire. More steps, set between two very fine petticoat palms (*Washingtonia filifera*), descend to the swimming pool on the far side of a large lawn. Here the garden becomes more tropical, with enormous specimens of *Agave ferox* brandishing fearsome looking spines, a beautiful pink-flowered *Oreocereus celsianus*, several clumps of Egyptian paper reed (*Cyperus papyrus*), a number of Canary Island date palms (*Phoenix canariensis*), some *Agave striata*, a variety of New Zealand flax (*Phormium tenax* 'Variegatum'), with long, yellow and green striped leaves, magnificent *Strelitzia nicolai* with huge white flowers like mythical birds, splendid specimens of *Cycas revoluta*, *Butia capitata*, and *Grevillea robusta*, which is covered with unusual yellow flowers in June.

Lemon trees, their leaves thick and glossy like most of the citrus trees of Sicily, grow here in profusion, marking the way to a track lined with spiny plants such as *Nopalea cochenillifera*, *Opuntia stricta* and *Euphorbia candelabrum*, which form an impenetrable barrier. The route towards the house passes through a group of Aleppo pines (*Pinus halepensis*), *Ulmus pumila*, and white poplars (*Populus alba*): the soil here is ideally suited to the poplars, which grow wild in this area.

Behind the house is a superb rose garden, raised and separated from the rest of the garden by a wall entirely covered with 'Clair Matin' roses and hedged in at the bottom by 'Albéric Barbier'. Orange and other fruit trees at the center rise above a broad carpet of multicolored roses bounded by a hedge of *Salvia officinalis*: the overall effect is quite delightful. The rose varieties have been carefully chosen to provide continuous flowering in May and June and from September to January. A small courtyard leads through an old gateway, once used for carriges, to the main entrance of the house; close by is the ancient chapel of San Andrea, surrounded by specimens of *Schinus molle*, known as pepper trees because of the pungent aroma given off by their leaves.

PHOENIX CANARIENSIS AND OTHER PALMS SURROUND THE POOL SIDE.

Principessa Miki Borghese's extremely wide knowledge of tropical and semi-tropical plants is what makes Il Biviere so unusual and so individual. Gardens should bear the stamp of their creator, and here the expertise and attention devoted to succulents, the princess's particular passion, give the place its own identity and character. The garden has never been laid out according to any particular plan, but has developed gradually and almost of its own accord: gardeners in Sicily are in a very privileged position as the climate allows them to grow a variety of rare plants from north Africa, the south of Spain, and practically all the countries that border the Mediterranean. It is a real delight to recognize the same plants in very different locations, and to see the similarities that exist between one tropical or semi-tropical garden and another. The gardens of Sicily are closely linked to those of the Arab world both through history and through climate. Certainly Sicilian gardens have developed a more European style over the centuries, but they have never entirely abandoned the legacy of the Arabs, a legacy of scented plants, fruit trees with citruses, and the sound of running water, and above all the sort of intoxicating exotic profusion that makes the gardens of Il Biviere so spectacular.

ABOVE: Xanthorrhoea arborea
LEFT: Trichocereus
(Torch cactus)
Far left: Deep scarlet
bougainvilleas run along one
side of the villa.

Bibliography

Bonomelli, *Il Papi in Campagna*
Casini Editore, Roma 1953

Cerio, Edwin, *Flora Privata on Capri*
Napoli 1939

Dami, Luigi, *Il Nostro Giardino*
Felice Monnior Editore, Firenze 1923

D'Harcourt, Duc, *Des Jardines Heureux*
Robert Baffon, Paris 1989

De Ligne Chartes, Joseph, *Il Giardini di Beloeil*
Sellerro Editore, Palermo 1985

Hortus Third, *L.H. Bailey Hortorium*
Cornell University, New York,
London 1978

Majnoni, Francesco, *La Badia a Coltibuono*
Francesco Papafava Editore, Firenze 1981

Masson, Georgina, *Italian Gardens*
Thames and Hudson, London 1961

Origo, Iris, *Images and Shadows*
John Murray, London 1970

The Royal Horticultural Society,
Dictionary of Gardening
Clarendon Press, Oxford 1984

Sitwell, Sir George
Sitwell, Sacheverell
Sitwell, Osbert
Sitwell, Reresby,
Hortus Sitwellianus
Michael Russell Publishing Ltd,
London 1984

Taverna, Lavinia, *Un Giardino Mediterraneo*
Rizzoli Editore, Milano 1982

Walton, Susan, *William Walton, Behind the Façade*
Oxford University Press, Oxford 1988

Plant Index